Malta

WHAT'S NEW | WHAT'S ON | WHAT'S BEST

www.timeout.com

Contents

Malta by Area

Essentials

Published by Time Out Guides Ltd
Universal House
251 Tottenham Court Road
London W1T 7AB
Tel: + 44 (0)20 7813 3000
Fax: + 44 (0)20 7813 6001
Email: guides@timeout.com
www.timeout.com

Managing Director Peter Fiennes
Financial Director Gareth Garner
Editorial Director Ruth Jarvis
Deputy Series Editor Dominic Earle
Editorial Manager Holly Pick
Assistant Management Accountant Ija Krasnikova

Time Out Guides is a wholly owned subsidiary of Time Out Group Ltd.

© Time Out Group Ltd
Chairman Tony Elliott
Financial Director Richard Waterlow
Group General Manager/Director Nichola Coulthard
Time Out Magazine Ltd MD Richard Waterlow
Time Out Communications Ltd MD David Pepper
Time Out International Ltd MD Cathy Runciman
Production Director Mark Lamond
Group IT Director Simon Chappell
Head of Marketing Catherine Demajo

Time Out and the Time Out logo are trademarks of Time Out Group Ltd.

This edition first published in Great Britain in 2008 by Ebury Publishing
A Random House Group Company
Company information can be found on www.randomhouse.co.uk
10 9 8 7 6 5 4 3 2 1

Distributed in US by Publishers Group West
Distributed in Canada by Publishers Group Canada

For further distribution details, see www.timeout.com

ISBN: 978-1-84670-078-1

A CIP catalogue record for this book is available from the British Library

Printed and bound by Firmengruppe APPL, aprinta druck, Wemding, Germany

The Random House Group Limited supports The Forest Stewardship Council (FSC), the
leading international forest certification organisation. All our titles that are printed on
Greenpeace approved FSC certified paper carry the FSC logo. Our paper procurement
policy can be found at www.rbooks.co.uk/environment.

Time Out carbon-offsets all its flights with Trees for Cities (www.treesforcities.org).

All rights reserved. No part of this publication may be reproduced, stored in a
retrieval system, or transmitted in any form or by any means, electronic, mechanical,
photocopying, recording or otherwise, without prior permission from the copyright owners.

Malta Shortlist

The **Time Out Malta Shortlist** is one of a new series of guides that draws on Time Out's background as a magazine publisher to keep you current with what's going on locally. As well as Malta and Gozo's key sights and the best of their eating, drinking and leisure options, the guide picks out the most exciting venues to have recently opened and gives a full calendar of annual events. It also includes features on the important news, trends and essentials compiled by locally based editors and writers. Whether you're visiting for the first time, or you're a regular, you'll find the *Time Out Malta Shortlist* contains all you need to know in a portable and easy-to-use format.

The guide divides the islands into seven area chapters, each of which contains listings for Sights & Museums, Eating & Drinking, Shopping, Nightlife and Arts & Leisure, with maps pinpointing the locations of those venues listed. At the front of the book are chapters rounding up these scenes island-wide, and giving a shortlist of our overall picks in a variety of categories. We also include itineraries for days out, plus essentials such as transport information, local resources and a list of the best hotels across both of the islands and covering a range of budgets.

Our listings give all phone numbers as dialled within Malta. The international code is 356; to call from outside Malta, follow this with the number given.

We have also noted price categories by using one to four € signs (€-€€€€), representing budget, moderate, expensive and luxury. Major credit cards are accepted unless otherwise stated. We have also indicated when a venue is NEW.

All our listings are double-checked, but Malta has a rather fluid attitude to retail, entertainment and hospitality, and places do sometimes close or change their hours or prices, so it's wise to call a venue before visiting. While every effort has been made to ensure accuracy, the publishers cannot accept responsibility for any errors that this guide may contain.

Venues are marked on the maps using symbols numbered according to their order within the chapter and colour-coded according to the type of venue they represent:

➊ Sights & Museums
➊ Eating & Drinking
➊ Shopping
➊ Nightlife
➊ Arts & Leisure

Map key

Major sight or landmark	▬
Railway station	▬
Park	▬
Pedestrian zone	▬
Church	✚
Steps	▬

Time Out Malta Shortlist

EDITORIAL
Editor Cyrus Shahrad
Copy Editor Jonathan Derbyshire
Proofreader Tamsin Shelton
Map Checker Claire Azzopardi
Indexer Rob Norman

DESIGN
Art Director Scott Moore
Art Editor Pinelope Kourmouzoglou
Senior Designer Henry Elphick
Graphic Designers Gemma Doyle,
  Kei Ishimaru
Digital Imaging Simon Foster
Advertising Designer Jodi Oher
Picture Editor Jael Marschner
Deputy Picture Editor Katie Morris
Picture Researcher Gemma Walters
Picture Desk Assistant Marzena Zoladz

ADVERTISING
Commercial Director Mark Phillips
International Advertising Manager
  Kasimir Berger
International Sales Executive Charlie Sokol
Advertising Sales (Malta) Content House Ltd
Advertising Assistant Kate Staddon

MARKETING
Marketing Manager Yvonne Poon
Senior Publishing Brand Manager
  Luthfa Begum
**Sales & Marketing Director,
  North America** Lisa Levinson
Marketing Designers Anthony Huggins,
  Nicola Wilson

PRODUCTION
Production Manager Brendan McKeown
Production Controller Damian Bennett
Production Co-ordinator Julie Pallot

CONTRIBUTORS
This guide was researched and written by Victor Borg, Jo Caruana,
Fiona Galea Debono, Deana Luchia, Ariadne Massa and Cyrus Shahrad.

PHOTOGRAPHY
All photography by Rene Rossignaud, except: pages 24, 25, 26, 28, 30, 32, 34,
36, 37, 48, 49, 52, 57, 58, 59, 60, 63, 67, 70, 76, 83, 86, 91, 94, 95, 99, 103,
110, 111, 112, 114, 117, 121, 122, 123, 127, 128, 130, 131, 132 Time Out Malta;
page 31 Gino Galea/Time Out Malta; page 79 Richie Abela; page 97 Marija Schranz.

The following images were provided by the featured establishments/artists:
pages 136, 141, 142, 143, 144, 149.

Cover © Pictures Colour Library.

MAPS
John Scott, JS Graphics (john@jsgraphics.co.uk). The maps of Malta, Gozo & Comino,
Valletta, Mdina and Victoria (Rabat) are based on material supplied by ITMB Vancouver.
The maps of St Julian's & Paceville, the Three Cities, Sliema and Rabat are based
on material supplied by Netmaps.

Thanks to Jesmond and Isabel at Content House Ltd.

About Time Out

Founded in 1968, Time Out has expanded from humble London beginnings into the leading
resource for those wanting to know what's happening in the world's greatest cities. As well
as our influential what's-on weeklies in London, New York and Chicago, we publish more
than a dozen other listings magazines in cities as varied as Beijing and Mumbai. The
magazines established Time Out's trademark style: sharp writing, informed reviewing
and bang up-to-date inside knowledge of every scene.

Time Out made the natural leap into travel guides in the 1980s with the City Guide
series, which now extends to over 50 destinations around the world. Written and
researched by expert local writers and generously illustrated with original photography,
the full-size guides cover a larger area than our Shortlist guides and include many
more venue reviews, along with additional background features and a full set of maps.

Throughout this rapid growth, the company has remained proudly independent, still
owned by Tony Elliott four decades after he started Time Out London as a single
fold-out sheet of A5 paper. This independence extends to the editorial content of all
our publications, this Shortlist included. No establishment has been featured because
it has advertised, and no payment has influenced any of our reviews. And, for our critics,
there's definitely no such thing as a free lunch: all restaurants and bars are visited and
reviewed anonymously, and Time Out always picks up the bill.
For more about the company, see www.timeout.com.

Don't Miss

St John's Co-Cathedral

Sights & Museums

Few places offer sights covering quite so comprehensive a cross-section of history as Malta – from Neolithic burial chambers and Roman ruins to the grand Baroque buildings forming the legacy of the Knights of St John. On top of this there are numerous museums exploring the cultural development of the islands and various more interactive attractions catering to younger audiences through the use of film, computer graphics and even live actors. Within any given city or area, most sights will be within walking distance of each other, and admission prices are cheap enough to allow visitors to take in several in one day.

Valletta

Topping most tour itineraries is grand St John's Co-Cathedral (p56),

densely packed with the tombs of individual Knights and embellished with dramatic Baroque reliefs and atmospheric paintings, including Caravaggio's masterpiece *The Beheading of St John the Baptist*. Yet more Knightly riches are on display at the Grand Master's Palace & Armoury (p52), seat of power since its establishment in 1571 and site of the Maltese presidential office to this day; its five State Rooms, which are open to the public, are filled with lustrous fittings, elaborately gilded ceilings and frescoes depicting the Knights in battle, as well as more recent portraits of British monarchs installed during colonial rule.

Valletta is also teeming with churches, including the Jesuits Church (p53), Our Lady of Mount Carmel and Our Lady of Victory (both p56), the latter founded to celebrate success in the Great Siege of 1565 and originally serving as the Knights' main place of worship before the construction of St John's Co-Cathedral. Also worth a visit is St Paul's Shipwreck Church (p56), a tribute to the saint's conversion of the island following his shipwreck here in AD 60, and famously home to both the stone pillar on which he was beheaded and a fragment of his wrist bone set in a gold reliquary.

For those seeking enlightenment as well as inspiration, Valletta is also home to several museums, among the finest of which is the National Museum of Archaeology (p55), a repository for relics dating back to the Neolithic era that have over the centuries been unearthed on this most richly historical of islands. A short walk away is the National Museum of Fine Arts (p55), which displays works by artistic masters from the Italian Baroque painter Mattia Preti to Britain's Edward Lear. Other museums concern themselves with Malta's resilience during the bombing of World War II (pp36-38): these are the Lascaris War Rooms (p53), the National War Museum (p55) and the Wartime Experience (p57).

The last of these is a 45-minute documentary that's indicative of a trend towards less dry and dusty historical narratives across the capital, from the audio-visual walk-through of the Great Siege of Malta & the Knights of St John (p52) to the Knights Spectacular 1565 (p53), a reconstruction of the original battle for Malta featuring costume-clad actors and nail-biting action.

The Three Cities & around

Vittoriosa, Senglea and Cospicua, also known as the Three Cities, are characterised by old Baroque townhouses towering over narrow,

SHORTLIST

Houses of the holy
- Mosta Dome (p118)
- St John's Co-Cathedral (p56)
- St Mary's Cathedral (p126)
- St Paul's Cathedral (p107)

Remembering the war
- Lascaris War Rooms (p53)
- Malta At War Museum (p87)
- Malta Aviation Museum (p118)
- National War Museum (p55)

Truly tranquil gardens
- Casa Rocca Piccola (p49)
- Palazzo Parisio & Gardens (p118)
- San Anton Gardens (p119)

Mighty fine forts
- Fort Rinella (p84)
- Fort St Angelo (p84)
- Fort St Elmo (p49)

Visual thrills and spills
- The Great Siege of Malta & the Knights of St John (p52)
- The Knights Spectacular 1565 (p53)

Best museums
- Maritime Museum (p87)
- National Museum of Archaeology (p55)
- National Museum of Fine Arts (p55)

Underground wonders
- Ghar Dalam Cave & Museum (p122)
- Mdina Dungeons (p106)
- St Paul's Catacombs (p106)

Ancient altars
- Ggantija Temples (p130)
- Hagar Qim (p122)
- Hal Saflieni Hypogeum (p87)
- Mnajdra Temples (p122)

A peep inside the palace
- Grand Master's Palace & Armoury (p52)
- Inquisitor's Palace (p87)
- Palazzo Falson (p106)

DON'T MISS

MEXX

Baystreet Complex, Level 1, St. George's Bay, St. Julians STJ3315. **Valletta**, Republic Street, Valletta VLT1114I. **Mosta**, 67, Constitution Street, Mosta MST9058

MEXX.COM

National Museum of Fine Arts p9

meandering streets – Cospicua, virtually levelled in World War II, decidedly less so than the others – but Vittoriosa is the only one home to attractions of real cultural interest. Several of these can be found along the city's Waterfront (itself the site of a significant regeneration project in recent years), including Fort St Angelo (p84), an early bastion of the Knightly fortification of Malta, the splendid St Lawrence Church (p89) and the Maritime Museum (p87), home to countless artefacts salvaged from historical wrecks off the Maltese coast. There's also a chance to explore the subterranean air raid shelters, in which every resident of the Three Cities once cowered under a deluge of bombs, at the Malta At War Museum, while the Inquisitor's Palace (both p87) offers an insight into the power of the religious authorities in Malta.

It's also well worth travelling beyond the Three Cities to a series of sights in outlying settlements, including the ancient Hal Saflieni Hypogeum (p87) and the Tarxien Temples (p89), both found in Paola, and Fort Rinella in Kalkara (p84), an erstwhile Victorian fort built to house the Armstrong 100-ton gun, the largest cannon of all time.

Mdina & Rabat

The walled settlement of Mdina remains one of the best-preserved Baroque cities on earth, its small handful of streets lined with ornate townhouses and its central square dominated by St Paul's Cathedral (p107), the towering edifice of which was created by the Maltese master Lorenzo Gafa, while the Cathedral Museum (p104), across the street, is home to a good range of exhibits including a number of sublime woodcuts by Albrecht Dürer. And there are two more excellent museums in town: the Museum of Natural History (p106), with exhibitions expounding the evolution of local flora and fauna, and Palazzo Falson (p106), a 13th-century house filled with artefacts that provide a look at the lives of Maltese nobles through the ages.

It was from subterranean St Paul's Grotto (p108) that the saint is reputed to have preached to and baptised the islanders at large following his shipwreck. Indeed, many of the area's most intriguing sights are found not on the city streets, but beneath them. Mdina Dungeons (p106) come horribly to life with waxwork reconstructions of historical torture methods, while St Paul's Catacombs and St Agatha's Catacombs (both p106), which lie beneath the neighbouring overspill settlement of Rabat, served as places of illegal Christian interment under repressive Roman rule, and to this day their haunting halls and rock-cut chapels are filled with tombs and lined with stone sarcophagi (pp39-41). The Roman age of Rabat is also on display at the Domus Romana (p106), an excavated Roman house dating back to AD 50 and the site of a museum of related antiquities.

The rest of Malta

There's little in the way of cultural attractions to be discovered in the rather touristy coastal resorts of the north – the Church of Our Lady of Mellieha, St Paul's Shipwreck Church and Wignacourt Tower (all p111) are notable exceptions. More central Mosta, however, is well worth a visit, home as it is to the looming church known locally as the Mosta Dome (p118), which took on the mantle of the miraculous when a World War II bomb fell through the roof and landed in the middle of the congregation during mass, but failed to explode. There's more airborne wartime interest at the nearby Malta Aviation Museum (p118), built on the former Ta' Qali airfield, while the grounds of the Palazzo Parisio & Gardens (p118), in neighbouring Naxxar, offer a relaxing place to unwind. Also eminently unstressful is a day wandering the Three Villages of Lija, Balzan and Attard (pp42-45), the last of which is home to the tranquil San Anton Gardens (p119).

Ancient history buffs will want to make a bee-line straight for the major Neolithic temples of southeastern Qrendi: Hagar Qim comprises a circular complex of chambers, while the nearby

Mnajdra Temples (both p122) are smaller and more intimate, built symmetrically and home to various semi-collapsed altars. Also offering a unique insight into Malta's more ancient days is the Ghar Dalam Cave & Museum (p122), which showcases remains and relics excavated from a single cave stretching 144 metres (472 feet) into the bedrock and more than 500,000 years into the past.

Gozo & Comino

Malta's sister island is more rural and less touched by the Baroque hand of the Knights, but still has a fair share of historical attractions, most of them located in the looming citadel of the central town of Victoria (also known as Rabat). These include Lorenzo Gafa's magnificent St Mary's Cathedral (p126), the interior of which has a convincing trompe l'oeil to convey the impression of an exterior dome that was never completed. There are also the reconstructed cells of the 16th-century Old Prison (p126) and the Archaeology Museum (p123), the latter filled with relics illuminating various civilisations that called the island home, from the Neolithic temple builders and Romans to the Knights themselves.

The work of those same temple builders can be seen elsewhere in Gozo at the staggering Ggantija Temples in Xaghra (p130), the still standing altars of which date back to 3600 BC and shed an interesting light on the 'Fat Lady' fertility cult that once worshipped here. More conventional places of worship come in the form of San Dimitri Chapel and Ta' Pinu Basilica in Gharb (both p130), the former built on the site of Malta's favourite legend, the latter set in open fields on the spot where Jesus reputedly appeared to a local peasant, and a place of pilgrimage to this day.

Zest p14

Eating & Drinking

Despite Malta's close proximity to Sicily, its inhabitants have yet to master their neighbours' art of creating consistently delectable food from the freshest ingredients. Malta is teeming with restaurants, but a great many still survive on turning out unimaginative pizza and pasta dishes from identikit Mediterranean menus.

This doesn't mean that you won't eat well, nor will you pay through the nose for the privilege: prices vary dramatically, with fresh fish and good wine pushing up the final bill, but it is possible for two people to enjoy a decent dinner with wine for around €50 (although expect to tip between ten to 15 per cent for good service). In our restaurant reviews we've broken venues down as budget (average main course below €7), moderate (€7-€15), expensive (€15-€20) and luxury (above €20) – divisions marked € to €€€€ respectively – although you'll see surprisingly few examples of this last category.

Good meals can be had anywhere in Malta, but meals that truly blow you away are less easy to come by – a great lunch or dinner here has as much to do with fantastic sea views as it does with the food itself. The popular dining strips along Spinola Bay in St Julian's, Valletta Waterfront, Vittoriosa's Grand Harbour or in Gozo's Marsalforn are big on panoramic vistas of boat-filled bays, but short on cooking that lingers in the memory any longer than it does the mouth.

Trabuxu p17

Cooking up a storm

Great restaurants and imaginative chefs do exist here, they're just few and far between. And to find them you'll have to wean yourself off those ubiquitous alfresco terraces and settle for dining indoors.

For fresh fish try Fumia (p58) – a Sicilian restaurant that's located beneath Valletta's Manoel Theatre and popular with after-show diners. If it's Asian cuisine you're after, try Taste (p96), a great Vietnamese fusion restaurant in Sliema, or Zest in St Julian's (p80), which has a broader Asian menu that includes Japanese, Thai and Indonesian dishes. Giuseppi's Wine Bar & Restaurant in Mellieha (p113) is considered by many to be one of the island's best restaurants: small and intimate, and set in a charming old two-storey villa, its menu offers an innovative take on Italian fare, featuring enigmatic specials by renowned chef Michael Diacono (rabbit with chocolate sauce is a perennial favourite). Over in Attard, Etienne Locum Vinim (p119) has a modern Mediterranean menu and over 300 well-selected

wines, with regular wine tastings as well as a six-course *menu degustazione* for those who prefer to tantalise their taste buds rather than overwhelm them.

Finally, don't be put off by the location of Essence (p113), set in the five-star Radisson SAS Golden Sands Resort and Spa; this really is one of Malta's finest restaurants, with an imaginative menu and a laid-back ambience bolstered by the acoustic guitarist strumming away laconically in one corner. It's hardly the place to come for traditional Maltese cuisine, but for top-end food with ocean views it simply can't be beaten.

Not that you should completely ignore the local culinary culture. Vegetarians and calorie counters may faint at the prospect, but for the rest of us a trip to Malta isn't complete without a taste of traditional Maltese cooking. Typical dishes include rabbit cooked in a tomato sauce or fried with garlic; the carbohydrate-heavy *timpana* (baked macaroni with a bolognese sauce topped with a lid of pastry); and 'beef olives' (thin slices of beef rolled around a filling of minced beef, carrot, boiled egg and parsley). While many restaurants have typical Maltese dishes on their menu, there's an almost island-wide reluctance to create great or ground-breaking dishes from traditional Maltese staples. A safe bet, however, is Ta' Marija in Mosta (p120), eminently popular with both locals and tourists for its traditional food and accompanying Maltese folk dancing and singing. Rubino in Valletta (p62), meanwhile, single-handedly spearheads a campaign for the preservation of Maltese recipes through the generations.

Tipples with taste

One interesting trend delivering a much-needed breath of fresh air to Malta's dining scene in recent years is the emergence of wine bars serving food. Such venues tend to be small and tucked away down hidden or half-forgotten alleys – something that only adds to their charm in the minds of most visitors – and the best of them have succeeded in tempting previously resigned diners off their sofas and out to sample the islands' cuisine.

Menus are limited, but these bars serve some delicious snack-style food – from imaginative dips (think beetroot rather than hummus) and wonderful Maltese platters (mixing local *bigilla* bean dip and crackers, sharp Gozitan *gbejnet* cheese with peppers and spiced sausage) to full-blown meals. The medieval city of Vittoriosa is a great place to go wine bar-hopping, its narrow, plant-pot lined alleyways oozing history and character and studded with excellent venues. One of the first and still among the best is Del Borgo (p90), boasting a fantastic location in a centuries-old cellar complete with stone arches and warm wooden beams. Just around

DON'T MISS

SHORTLIST

Best new restaurants
- Spezzo (p62)
- Two and a Half Lemon (p90)

Terrific terraces
- Café Luna (p119)
- Country Terrace (p131)
- Ristorante Venezia (p90)

Eastern promise
- Blue Elephant (p73)
- Shiva's (p77)
- Taste (p96)

Traditional Maltese delights
- Rubino (p62)
- Ta' Kris (p96)
- Ta' Marija (p120)

Great pizza and pasta
- La Cuccagna (p95)
- Piccolo Padre (p76)
- Tal-Kaptan (p115)

Best hotel restaurants
- Essence (p113)
- Zest (p80)

Eating on the cheap
- Café Barrakka (p57)
- Café Jubilee (p58, p126)
- Mgarr Ix-Xini Kiosk (p133)

Something fishy
- Barracuda (p73)
- Fumia (p58)
- Otters (p133)

Wine bars with bottle
- L'Angolo di Vino (p89)
- Del Borgo (p90)
- Castille Wine Vaults (p58)
- Il-Forn (p90)
- Trabuxu (p62)

Drink beer, fall over
- Blackbull (p73)
- Huggins (p75)
- Ryan's Irish Bar (p77)

Bars with class
- b'art (p94)
- Quarterdeck Bar (p76)
- 2 22 (p62)

timeout.com

Over 50 of the world's greatest
cities reviewed in one site.

Time Out
Online

the corner is Il-Forn (p90), a large wine bar and restaurant that specialises in grilled *ftiras* (Maltese flat bread filled with pizza-style ingredients), plus salads, platters and pasta dishes complemented by a long wine list and some extremely potent sangrias. L'Angolo di Vino (p89), meanwhile, is the newest of Vittoriosa's wine bars, not to mention the smallest and most intimate, founded by Maltese broadcast journalist and noted wine authority Glenn Bedingfield.

Even sleepy Valletta has seen a boost in the number of its evening visitors thanks to the wine bar explosion. Deservedly popular is subterranean Trabuxu (p62), set in a 300-year-old cellar steeped in wine lore, its thick stone walls decorated with brass musical instruments and the occasional painting. A mostly 30-plus crowd gathers nightly to make the most of more than 300 wines and an accompanying menu offering snack platters and simple meals such as moussaka and lasagna, but reservations aren't taken, so get there early if you're hoping to bag a table. 2 22 (see p62) is another happening spot with a menu as well thought-out as its wine list, as is Legligin (p61), where indefatigable owner Chris Misfud Bonnici concocts culinary miracles on a two-burner stove.

Drinking to forget

Beyond foody wine bars, more discerning drinkers might well feel left out in the cold. The Maltese like a drink as much as the next nation and are deservedly proud of their locally produced beers and wines – Cisk and Hopleaf are popular examples of the former, while local grapes such as *gellewza*, *gennarua* and *ghirghentina* dominate in Maltese vineyards – but bars

without menus seem to have all but disappeared from the streets during recent years.

Needless to say there are still hundreds of pubs in the tourist-packed north of the island (and in Marsascala in the south), but there's nothing unmissable about the vast majority. St Julian's is widely considered the best of a bad bunch. The streets of Paceville are slightly squalid and/or wildly exciting depending on your age or inclination, packed with teenagers and twenty-somethings hell-bent on achieving alcohol-fuelled oblivion in a dense mass of bars and clubs, busy year round but packed to bursting thanks to an influx of EFL students in summer. Those wanting to sit rather than fall down of an evening should settle on the less abrasive Dusk Lounge Bar (p73) or Quarterdeck Bar (p76) – both catering to a more mixed age group – while Ryan's Irish Bar (p77) is popular with the younger crowd thanks to its upbeat DJs and dancefloor, the latter lubricated by jugs of Red Bull and vodka in more ways than one.

Ta' Marija p15

Marsaxlokk p22

WHAT'S BEST
Shopping

Shopping in Malta was a very different experience until as recently as the late 1980s. Before then, a government determined to promote local products enforced a blanket ban on various foreign imports. While the ban was in place, the Maltese would regularly return from trips abroad carrying suitcases loaded with Mars bars, Colgate toothpaste and clothing from labels that couldn't be found on the islands. If they made it back through customs, they became the heroes of both friends and family.

Not so today. Malta's accession to the EU has helped speed up retail evolution, as did its adoption, in January 2008, of the euro, and the current situation sees Malta teeming with international brands,

many of them sold from official branches in the capital and beyond. Now locals can finally lay their hands on whatever their hearts desire – from designer clothes and shoes to electronics, jewellery and stylish homeware.

But that's not to say that the islands are now bereft of uniquely Maltese shopping experiences: local handicrafts abound, plus there has been a marked resurgence in the popularity of local brands and products including beer, wine and olive oil (see box p88). Nor will you be forced to shop in bland malls or on tawdry high streets: for the most part, even established international brands can now be found operating out of charmingly traditional Maltese houses.

A word of warning: newsagents aside, shopping on Sundays is practically unheard of in Malta, a nation that wears its Catholicism on its sleeve, and several attempts to introduce the concept have been quashed by shopkeepers hoping to keep the Sabbath day holy – ironic, seeing as even the most pious seem to succumb to the festive spirit of shameless materialism and keep their shutters open seven days a week in the run-up to Christmas.

However, those determined to splash the cash on Sundays will find salvation at the Bay Street Complex in St Julian's (p80), which is open on Sundays and public holidays from 10am to 10pm, and which houses a range of international fashion outlets including Mexx, Guess, French Connection and Tommy Hilfiger, plus 16 stores selling everything from jewellery and make-up to toys, perfumes and wines.

Capital ideas

For a more authentically Maltese shopping experience, most visitors head straight to the historic capital Valletta, where the streets are lined with stores set in buildings dating all the way back to the Knights of St John. The main shopping strip is Triq Ir-Repubblica, where branches of international chains jostle for space with more traditional local outlets, many retaining their quaint wooden façades and authentic feel of centuries past.

Jewellery seekers are well served by a range of shops – from chains such as Classic Jewellers (p65) and Diamonds International (p65) to the family-run Victor Azzopardi Jewellers (p69) – many of them selling pieces by global designers such as Bulgari and Chaumet alongside own- and locally-made creations (gold and silver Maltese crosses remain big sellers).

S H O R T L I S T

For Maltese handicrafts
- Artisans Centre (p63)
- Mdina Glass (p67)
- Ta' Dbiegi Crafts Centre (p143)
- Ta' Qali Crafts Village (p120)

Jewellers in the crown
- Bejewelled (p98)
- Edwards Lowell Co Ltd (p66)
- Victor Azzopardi Jewellers (p69)

Food for thought
- Carmelo Micallef Bakery (p98)
- C Camilleri & Sons Ltd (p65)
- Est Est Est (p99)

Designers for life
- Ascot House (p63)
- De Fort Designerwear (p80)
- Kenjo & Kyoto (p66)

Main shopping centres
- Arkadia Commercial Centre (p128)
- Bay Street Complex (p80)
- Embassy Complex (p66)
- Plaza Shopping Centre (p101)

Sporting chances
- Friction (p80)
- TeamSport (p102)
- Urban Jungle (p102)

Homeware the heart is
- Cleland & Souchet (p80)
- Eighteen-Ninety by Camilleri Paris Mode (p99)
- Junction 66 (p100)

Best for kids
- Early Learning Centre (p65)
- Pedigree Toyshops (p68)

Holiday reading resources
- Agenda Bookshop (p63)
- Books Plus (p98)
- Sapienza's Bookshop (p68)

Bags of style
- Jeannine (p100)
- Porto (p80)

DON'T MISS

www.visitMALTA.com

you're virtually there!

Should you be feeling 'under the weather', a visit to the all-new, all-inclusive, one-stop web portal for anything and everything about Malta, Gozo & Comino will definitely put you in a better mood.

Whether abroad or in Malta, immerse yourself in all you need to know about the heart of the Mediterranean. **www.visitmalta.com** virtually spoils you for choice with things to do and places to visit in the Maltese islands.

BOOK ON-LINE
AT THE OFFICIAL E-PORTAL FOR MALTA, GOZO & COMINO

MALTA
MALTA GOZO COMINO

Valletta is also a good place to come for traditional Maltese crafts, from majestic hand-painted wall clocks (see box p64) to blown glass ornaments and intricate lacework; the Artisans Centre (p63) and Mdina Glass (p67) are both great spots to pick up gifts. And there's plenty of big brand fashion to be found too, from Morgan and Miss Sixty to Mexx (all three p67) and Mango (p66).

Triq Il-Merkanti competes heavily for custom, with a recent and much-needed facelift having enticed numerous new businesses. The Diesel Store (p65) and Early Learning Centre (p65) are among the better-known brands currently calling the strip home, although you'll also find more traditional treats from C Camilleri & Sons Ltd (p65), a centuries-old confectioner turning out every kind of Maltese sweet under the sun (see box p109).

Lastly, for a real bargain, check out the local flea market operating in the mornings from Monday to Saturday midway down Triq Il-Merkanti, and offering everything from cheap homeware and knock-off designer bags to costume jewellery and clothing. Recent police efforts to crack down on illegal CD and DVD sellers have been half-hearted to say the least, and the market is still teeming with the latest major label releases and Hollywood blockbusters – many of the latter decidedly grainier than the studios intended.

With very few exceptions, shops in Valletta tend to open between 9am and 1pm, at which point they close for a siesta before reopening from 4pm to 7pm.

Style for sale

It may lack Valletta's old-world charm, but the affluent coastal town of Sliema certainly packs a commercial punch.

Carmelo Micallef Bakery p22

The majority of cash changes hands along two main shopping streets, Triq Bisazza and the Strand, which between them offer over 600 outlets, many of them selling the latest international designer wear – from clothes and shoes to accessories. High street chains include the likes of Next (p101), Wallis (p102) and Max Mara (p100), giving the streets of Sliema a more mainland European flavour and a cosmopolitan air bolstered by its well-heeled patrons – from elegantly dressed men-about-town to designer-clad ladies-who-lunch, many of them doing exactly that on sun-drenched café terraces.

A third main retail stretch, Triq It-Torri, is big on trendy boutiques and jewellery stores – including a new branch of diamante specialist Swarovski (p102) – but it's rather sadly choked with fumes from a ceaseless flow of traffic. It's still worth the trip, however, to drop in on Est Est Est (p99), an upmarket delicatessen offering a wide range of speciality foods, sweets, wines, champagnes and artisan teas – a real godsend on an island where turning up as a dinner guest without some sort of edible or quaffable gift is considered a big faux pas. There's also a good range of fine food and wine at Eighteen-Ninety by Camilleri Paris Mode (p99), a family-run store that also stocks an abundance of luxury home goods, from antique furniture to bed linen.

Finally, for an enjoyable break in the retail agenda, call in at Carmelo Micallef Bakery (p98), one of the oldest and most respected bread makers on an island devoted to the stuff – and never more so than when it's drizzled with olive oil and rubbed with fresh tomatoes (*hobz biz-zejt*). Grab some of the latter at the traditional fruit and vegetable stand at Dingli Circus (Triq Sir Adrian Dingli), and then stroll down to the nearby beach to indulge yourself with a picnic of simple Maltese fare.

Commodities culture

Malta is also home to several shopping experiences that are as unique in terms of their setting as the products they sell. Arguably most charismatic of all is the weekly fish market at Marsaxlokk (p121), a fishing village on the southeastern coast that turns into a hive of activity between 7am and 1pm every Sunday, its stalls overflowing with fresh swordfish, octopus, tuna and dorado – the latter, known locally as *lampuki*, a special in eateries across the island during summer. The fishermen set up stalls along the water's edge and are more than happy for tourists to poke around their haul and ask questions about the catch – just be sure to get there early, as buyers for local hotels and restaurants tend to have snapped up the best stuff by lunchtime.

Equally special is the Ta' Qali Crafts Village (p120), northeast of Mdina, in which local artisans – from carpenters to jewellers, metalworkers to lace makers – sell their wares out of refurbished Nissen huts on the former World War II airfield. A similar handicraft hub exists on Gozo at the Ta' Dbiegi Crafts Centre (p134), a cluster of workshops everything from blown glass to brassware, and which has been recently refurbished thanks to significant EU funding. Elsewhere, however, Gozo is less of a retail destination than its sister island, with shopping opportunities largely confined to the Arkadia Commercial Centre in Victoria (p128), home to a large supermarket and four floors offering branches of predictable household brands.

Paceville

Nightlife

In many ways, Malta's nightlife
scene perfectly embodies the laid-
back Mediterranean spirit: parties
start late and finish even later, and
each one is lived as if it were the last.

Admission to most venues is free
unless they're staging an organised
event, and while the law demands
that bars and clubs turn off their
music at 4am, they can continue
serving food and alcohol for 24
hours. An island-wide smoking ban
has been in force since 2004, adding
a conversational alfresco element
to even the noisiest night, and
the crowds tend to be young: the
legal age for alcohol consumption
in Malta is 16, while an annual
summer influx of international
English-language students helps
keep the average age down.

The pleasure principle

The scene is largely concentrated
in the St Julian's and Paceville area
on the island's northeastern coast,
with so dense a network of bars
and clubs (many of the former
featuring in-house DJs) that
bar hopping is slowly becoming
recognised as a kind of national
sport. A reputation for safe streets
and a minimal police presence
only adds to the atmosphere. It
goes without saying that nights
here can be as noisy as they are
freakishly fun, so while it's the
perfect place for twentysomethings
to call home for a couple of weeks,
families and couples would almost
certainly be better off choosing
accommodation in a more peaceful
part of the island.

Axis

It's not easy to keep abreast of the latest developments on the Paceville circuit: bars and clubs seem to be constantly being built or boarded up. Usually, though, it's a case of the same stalwarts re-inventing themselves: Axis (p81), for example, recently opened its doors as a superclub complete with a world-class PA and a programme boasting performances by major international DJs, but in fact it's one of Malta's oldest nightclubs, having brought techno and house to the island in the early 1990s.

The superclub format is not one you'll find repeated much across Malta: most venues are really clubby bars, sticking to a reliable mix of uptempo chart-toppers, cheesy classics and cheerful house music. But there are exceptions like Havana (p81), which is Malta's mecca for hip hop and R&B heads.

And there are other types of venue looking to take punters into the small hours. Gambling is big business, with popular spots including the Oracle Casino in Bugibba (p116), the Dragonara Casino Barrière in St Julian's (p82) and the Casino Di Venezia on Vittoriosa Waterfront (p90). On top of that, table-dancing clubs have become increasingly popular over the last few years, especially with British lad-packers – there are four such venues within a few square metres of each other in Paceville alone – while the popular explosion of upmarket wine bars caters to a more mature clientele that prefers drinks of distinction and music it can talk over, with Del Borgo and Il-Forn (both p90) in Vittoriosa among the most notable.

Party over here

For the most part, however, central Paceville is considered ground zero for good times in Malta, teeming with impossibly young and up-for-it punters on a nightly basis – but it's not just for the kids.

SHORTLIST

For raving alfresco
- Club Numero Uno (p120)
- Gianpula (p109)
- La Grotta (p134)

For classy clubbers
- Level 22 (p81)
- Molecule (p109)
- Shadow Lounge (p82)
- Styx (p82)

For a proper mash-up
- Axis (p81)
- Qube (p81)
- Sabor (p82)
- Sky Club (p82)
- Tattingers Club (p109)

For more eclectic music
- BJ's Nightclub (p81)
- Fuego Salsa Bar (p81)
- Havana (p81)

For clubbing by the water
- Amazonia Nightclub (p116)
- Beachaven (p116)

Hugo's Lounge (p75) is a great choice for more mature pleasure-seekers, a civilised one-stop shop where patrons can enjoy superb Asian cuisine in the ground-floor restaurant before moving upstairs to the contemporary lounge bar, and later – should the urge take them – proceeding up one flight further to the new Shadow Lounge (p82), a glamorous, glass-walled club with an eminently chilled vibe, a decent list of drinks and sweeping views of the chaotic, bar-choked streets down below.

Other clubs catering to more discerning crowds can be found in nearby St Julian's, with Level 22 (p81), on the 22nd floor of the smart Portomaso tower, among the most stunning, offering 360° views and attentive table service, and catering to a mix of upmarket locals and tourists from the neighbourhood's luxury hotels with an atmosphere of well-heeled exclusivity. The nearby Sky Club (p82) is another

new venue adding a dash of style to the clubbing scene, big on the usual laser-driven, hands-in-the-air house madness, but with a formidable VIP area with space for no fewer than 700 high-rollers.

For the most part, however, the VIP formula has never really worked in Malta: the crowds are so small and the number of competing venues so relatively high that it's hard to turn punters away, and you're more likely to be presented with free entrance and cheap drinks (€2 for a beer, €2.30 for a mixer) than any kind of elitist nonsense about your name not being down on the guestlist.

Reach for the lasers

The general Maltese reluctance to pay entry to a bar or club has also created something of a dearth of venues hosting live music – BJ's

Nightclub (p81), in Paceville, is a notable exception – and this despite the abundance of local bands making waves across the island and beyond. Instead it's left largely to the hectic summer festival circuit to fill in the blanks, with each year bringing a greater number of crazed and colourful events than the last. Many of these have a decidedly clubby feel, especially those with MTV at the helm: Malta has just signed a contract that will see it remain the official 'Isle of MTV' until 2010, with a raft of affiliated club and live band nights culminating in a massive concert in June (2007's instalment pulled in an audience of over 50,000).

If you've missed it, however, fear not: there are other massive raves held on a summer monthly basis at major clubs across the island, including Club Numero Uno in Ta' Qali (p120) and Gianpula/Molecule in Rabat (p109). Located as they are in more desolate stretches of the island,

such venues are reminiscent of old-fashioned Ibiza-style discos – built around converted farmhouses and capable of accommodating up to 4,000 revellers. It's no surprise, then, that they also host occasional nights from some of the biggest international club promoters – Pacha, Cream, Ministry of Sound, Godskitchen – not to mention some of the biggest DJs: everyone from Carl Cox and Paul Oakenfold to Tiesto, Erick Morillo and Boy George has visited the island at least once, and most of them return time and time again.

Finally, those visitors seeking a more conventional helping of sun, sea and sand with their evening shenanigans will find the northern resort of Bugibba happy to oblige, with its hotchpotch of coastal hotels and beachside bars bustling in summer, and its main square teeming with a mix of tourists all determined to enjoy themselves until the small hours. Rookie's Sports Bar & Grill (p115) boasts DJs and the occasional live band taking drinkers on until 3am daily, while Amazonia Nightclub (p116) is one of the island's true seaside venues – a beach club by day that transforms nightly into a decadent dancing spot complete with lagoon-style pools and exotic palms.

The bottom line is that Malta belies its diminutive size and has something to offer night owls of all persuasions – from saucer-eyed club kittens and cocktail-fuelled lounge lizards to gamblers, gangsters and boys and girls just looking to drink themselves into oblivion. Locals may wince at the increasingly lascivious reputation of its undisputed nightlife capital, Paceville, not to mention the noise, but with the bulk of the chaos largely contained, and so much else on offer elsewhere on the island, few visitors are complaining.

Club Numero Uno

National Philharmonic Orchestra p28

Arts & Leisure

Malta has never been known for its cutting-edge artistic endeavour, but its accession to the EU in 2004 – and an associated increase in arts funding – has left things looking decidedly rosier for creative souls across the islands. These days there's something happening to suit the culturally minded whatever their calling – from stage to screen, from canvas to chorus – and while it's unlikely to be on a scale to rival cities like London or Paris, it's almost always done with gusto and an unjaded passion for the process.

Flipping the script

While no professional theatre companies have set up shop here, the islands are home to a thriving amateur scene that regularly stages productions of a high standard. Performances tend to be fairly mainstream, although some companies have staged more controversial productions over the years: Unifaun Theatre (www.unifauntheatre.com) had *Explicit Polaroids*, which featured 'Russian go-go boys, AIDS cocktails and horny ghosts', while Actinghouse Productions (www.actinghouse productions.com) have in recent years performed a range of modern English-language classics including *A Streetcar Named Desire* and *The Lady from the Sea*.

Both companies often perform at the St James Cavalier Centre for Creativity in Valletta (p69), Malta's one-stop shop for the arts since its establishment at the turn of the millennium. A jack-of-all-trades (and master of most), the centre hosts performing and visual arts, and on any given evening you could stumble upon anything from a stage play to a classical music recital, art installation or dramatic workshop. The building itself is worth the visit alone, built by the Knights of St John following the Great Siege of 1565 and subjected to a restoration as imaginative as any of its artistic displays.

We are the music makers

Valletta is also home to Malta's national playhouse, the Manoel Theatre (p69), another gloriously refurbished creation of the Knights and one of the oldest working theatres in Europe. The number of contemporary and classical plays performed here seems to decline with each passing season: the programme still boasts the occasional dramatic flourish (adaptations of both *The Picture*

of Dorian Gray and *Steel Magnolias* were performed here in 2007/08 alongside a popular Christmas pantomime, but these days it's mostly dedicated to hosting classical music concerts.

Indeed, recent years have seen Malta reach dizzying new musical heights: its National Philharmonic Orchestra (www.maltaorchestra.com), now in its 40th year, appears to have undergone something of a makeover with its annual 'Orchestra Goes Pop' concerts, which pair classical musicians with well-known local singers for mainstream chart meltdowns that pull in punters of all ages – the success of the events also led to classical performances in 2008 featuring Beatles hits and movie soundtracks. A growing number of Maltese bands have also come on to the scene in recent years, from pop to prog to punk artists – a good place to catch them is BJ's Nightclub in Paceville (p81), Malta's leading venue for staging live bands and home to an enigmatic annual 100-hour music marathon (usually taking place in March, www.music-marathon.com), which sees local bands performing non-stop for days on end and proceeds going to charity. At the other end of the scale, Malta has recently played host to concerts by big name international artists, with Elton John, Sting and Bryan Adams among those making stops on the island as part of their sell-out world or European tours.

Culture comes to life

Don't worry if singing along to *Candle in the Wind* isn't your idea of fun: Malta also offers a range of festivals for rootsier, more culturally rewarding experiences. Barely a summer weekend seems to pass without a colourful celebration of the likes of local food, folklore

Manoel Theatre

or fireworks, and all are great excuses for a party. The daddy of them all is the Malta Arts Festival (p32), which runs for three weeks each July and showcases a variety of local and foreign talent across various disciplines, with numerous old buildings across the capital – many of them ordinarily off limits to the public – dolled up and used as venues. The festival also brings live music and a vivid celebratory atmosphere to the streets of Valletta, something that's often sorely lacking in the capital. For more on Maltese festivals and events, see pp30-34.

When it comes to cinematic screenings, meanwhile, Malta shows films in English concurrent with European calendars; those keen to explore will find smaller cinemas dotted all over the island, although the largest and most accessible is the Eden Cinema in St Julian's (p82), home to 17 screens showing films throughout the day and long into the evening. Elsewhere, the cinema in the St James Cavalier Centre is one of few places in Malta to promote foreign and arthouse movies.

Surf and turf

First impressions might lead visitors to assume that Malta is too hot for sports, but the island caters to active-types regardless of their discipline or levels of determination. Those seeking an outdoor workout should head to the Marsa Sports Club (p90), with facilities for tennis, squash, cricket and swimming along with Malta's only 18-hole golf course. The club also hosts the increasingly popular national pastime of rugby most weekends between October and May, although the lion's share of the island's affection for spectator sports is reserved for football

SHORTLIST

Sound stages
- Astra Theatre (p128)
- Aurora Theatre (p129)
- Manoel Theatre (p69)

Versatile venues
- Mediterranean Conference Centre (p69)
- St James Cavalier Centre for Creativity (p69)

Best for sports nuts
- Cynergi (p82)
- Gozo Sports Complex (p129)
- Marsa Sports Club (p90)

Play your cards right
- Casino Di Venezia (p90)
- Oracle Casino (p116)

Best for kids
- Mediterraneo Marine Park (p116)
- Popeye Village (p118)
- Splash & Fun Water Park (p118)

DON'T MISS

(www.maltafootball.com). There are huge followings for both small-scale kickarounds on pitches across the country and major national and international games at the National Stadium in Ta' Qali (p120).

Most sporting tourists, however, will be more interested in making the most of Malta's coastline. Diving is the most popular pastime by far, with various schools offering courses or accompanied dives to countless wrecks and underwater beauty spots (see box p132). That said, there are also a great many opportunities for more adrenalin-fuelled pursuits: Mellieha Bay is the best for windsurfing, while the Malta Wakeboarding School operates out of nearby Xemxija, and there are various other companies hiring out everything from kayaks and pedalos to jet skis and speedboats.

Calendar

Malta's population may be so small that event organisers regularly have to rely on tourists to break even, but the islands still boast a busy and hugely varied calendar of year-round events. As well as hosting a number of one-off concerts featuring international performers (recent visitors have included Andrea Bocelli and Bryan Adams), the long summer months bring a slew of outdoor attractions such as jazz and rock festivals, yacht and powerboat races, and beer and wine festivals. Being staunchly Catholic, a number of the islands' most vibrant and colourful events are religious feasts, with the vivid Easter parades among the most fascinating.

All dates highlighted in **bold** are public holidays.

January

Ongoing **Pantomime** (see Dec)

February

10 Feast of St Paul's Shipwreck
Valletta and other venues
The capital is strewn with paper as a statue of the saint is carried shoulder high through the streets; churches are packed and decked out in finery.

Mid Feb **Song for Europe Festival**
Mediterranean Conference Centre, p69
The festival to find Malta's entry for the annual Eurovision Song Contest is an event the whole country enjoys.

20-24 (2009) **Carnival**
Valletta, Floriana, Nadur (Gozo) and other venues
www.maltafestivals.com
The best of the celebrations are concentrated in Valletta and Floriana, with huge parades, colourful floats and costume-clad revellers crowding the streets. Nadur's take on Carnival has a more ominous feel (see box p34).

Mid-late Feb **Malta Marathon**
Mdina to Sliema
www.maltamarathon.com

These popular marathon and half-marathon events attract both local and international runners, with a course taking athletes through central Malta.

March

Mar/Apr (date varies)
Easter Processions
Various venues
One week before Good Friday (Our Lady of Sorrows), a statue of Mary is carried through the streets in a solemn procession, with some walking barefoot and others dragging chains behind them. Similar processions take place throughout Malta on Palm Sunday, Good Friday and Easter Sunday.

Mar/Apr (date varies)
European Film Festival
Various venues
A festival organised by European Commission representatives in Malta and featuring movies from member states. Films are shown throughout the islands and proceeds go to charity.

21 **Spring Equinox**
Mnajdra Temples, p122
Heritage Malta organises guided sunrise tours of the Megalithic temples to mark the spring equinox, when the sun's rays shine through the precise centre of the lower temple's main doorway. Numbers are strictly limited.

April

Ongoing Easter Processions, European Film Festival (for both, see Mar)

Mid Apr **National Mechanical Ground Fireworks Festival**
Location varies
A spectacularly noisy and colourful night with local fireworks makers competing for awards. See box p53.

Apr/June (date varies) **Gaiafest**
Ghajn Tuffieha
www.projectgaia.org
A festival promoting holistic living, with talks and workshops on subjects such as the environment, psychotherapy and yoga. There's a vegetarian buffet and stalls sell natural produce.

May

Ongoing Gaiafest (see Apr)

Early May **Malta International Fireworks Festival**
Location varies
www.maltafireworks.com
A festival featuring pyrotechnic wonders from local and international manufacturers (see box p53).

Early May **Malta Horticulture Fair**
San Anton Gardens, p119
A small gardening fair with prizes for the best entries, set in one of Malta's most peaceful and pretty public spaces.

Early-mid May
Earth Garden Festival
National Park, Ta Qali
A two-day festival of dance, theatre, art exhibitions and music concerts, with the overall aim of promoting environmental awareness across Malta.

Mid May **Ghanafest – Malta Mediterranean Folk Music Festival**
Argotti Gardens, Floriana
www.maltaculture.com
An event showcasing Malta's rich musical heritage with live performances of *ghana* (folksong) and *daqq tal-prejjem* (Maltese guitar music).

Easter Processions

DON'T MISS

June

Ongoing Gaiafest (see Apr)

Early June **UIM Powerboat
P1 World Championship**
Grand Harbour, Valletta
www.powerboatp1.com
The Maltese leg of the world championship, with the Grand Harbour making a fantastic backdrop.

Mid June
Malta Football Awards
Corinthia Palace, Attard
Broadcast live, this annual event sees local and international players commended at a popular awards ceremony.

29 **Mnarja**
Buskett Gardens and other venues
Folk festival celebrating the feast of Saints Peter and Paul. There are also horse and donkey races on the streets of Rabat and in Nadur, Gozo.

July

Early July **Malta Arts Festival**
Various venues
www.maltaculture.com
A three-week festival celebrating the arts with a mix of dance, theatre, music concerts and exhibitions.

Mid July **Malta International
Blues & Wine Festival**
Valletta Waterfront
www.bluesfestivalmalta.com
Wine tasting to a soundtrack of local and international blues bands and with a spectacular watery backdrop.

Mid-late July
Malta Jazz & Rock Festival
Grand Harbour, Valletta
www.nngpromotions.com
International and local musicians take part in this popular four-day event, which occurs annually.

Late July
Farsons Great Beer Festival
National Park, Ta' Qali
www.farsons.com/beerfestival
Held annually, this brewery-organised festival is also a fun musical event with around 40 live performances.

August

Early Aug (Malta)/Late Aug (Gozo)
Delicata Classic Wine Festival
Upper Barrakka Gardens,
Valletta/Nadur, Gozo
Local winery Delicata hosts this annual wine festival to coincide with the local grape harvest, featuring wine tasting, fine food and entertainment.

Malta Military Tattoo

DON'T MISS

15 Feast of the Assumption
Attard, Ghaxaq, Gudja, Mosta,
Mqabba, Qrendi, Victoria (Gozo)
The Feast of the Assumption (Santa
Marija) is celebrated in seven towns.

Mid Aug **Gozo Music Festival**
Gozo (location varies)
www.gozomusicfestival.com
A range of Maltese musicians plus a
major international artist perform at
this Gozitan musical gathering.

September

**8 Our Lady of
Victories/Victory Day**
Grand Harbour, Valletta
Commemorating both the birth of
Mary and the end of the wartime seige
of the islands, and with an afternoon
regatta in the Grand Harbour.

27-28 (2008)
Malta International Airshow
Various venues
www.maltaairshow.com
Stunning aerial stunts at a show organ-
ised by the Malta Aviation Society.

October

Early Oct **Notte Bianca**
Valletta (various venues)
www.nottebiancamalta.com
Valletta stays open until late with an
evening of music, dance, exhibitions,
re-enactments and traditional crafts.
Museums and churches also open late.

11-12 (2008)
Malta Military Tattoo
Malta Fairs and Convention Centre,
Ta Qali
www.maltamilitarytattoo.org
A military music extravaganza featur-
ing rousing marches from both Maltese
and international bands.

18-25 (2008)
Rolex Middle Sea Race
Marsamxett Harbour
www.rolexmiddlesearace.com
One of the yachting world's most
esteemed races starts and finishes in
Malta, taking in the Straits of Messina,
Pantelleria, Lampedusa and Stromboli.

20-31 (2009)
Festival Mediterranea
Astra Theatre, p128
www.mediterranea.com.mt

Annual Gozo event showcasing the
island's cultural and artistic activities.
There are musical performances, art
exhibitions, conferences and field trips,
all with a creative bent.

25 Oct-4 Nov (2008)
**Malta International Choir
Competition & Festival**
Various venues
Choral groups from around the world
perform in churches across the islands
in a competition that is also a festival
of world-class performances.

Late Oct **Grand Prix de Malte**
Valletta
www.grand-prix-de-malte.com
A colourful mix of classic cars zoom-
ing around the city centre in a *Wacky
Races*-style competition.

November

Ongoing Malta International
Choir Competition & Festival
(see Oct)

28-30 (2008) **Malta International
Challenge Marathon**
Various venues
www.maltamarathonchallenge.com
A three-day, three-stage marathon that
starts and ends in Rabat and draws
professional runners and punters alike.

December

Early-mid Dec
Bay Music Awards
Eden Arena, St George's Bay
www.edenleisure.com
Event celebrating local music, organ-
ised by national radio station 89.7 Bay.
Maltese solo artists and bands compete
across six award categories.

Early-mid Dec **Teatru Unplugged**
Manoel Theatre, p69
Light-hearted musical event featuring
a mix of live performances covering
everything from classically trained
pianists to rock bands.

Dec/Jan **Pantomime**
Manoel Theatre, p69
www.madc.biz
This annual event sells out early. As in
the best pantomime tradition, kids
laugh at the spectacle and adults at the
shrewd asides on local politics. Popular
with homesick British expats.

Village of the damned

Carnival time sees the dead walking
the streets of one tranquil Gozitan town.

Carnival brings out the same spirit in Malta as it does in the rest of the world, with residents decked out in colourful costumes and streets gridlocked with extravagant floats. But as the appointed hour approaches in the sleepy Gozitan town of Nadur, things begin to take on an altogether darker hue.

According to local lore, the macabre antics of the inhabitants of Nadur date back to medieval days, when the morbidly freakish, maladjusted and downright mad were kept hidden away, allowed out to mingle with the masses only on the rarest of occasions. **Nadur Carnival** (p30) provides a contemporary parallel for one such occasion, an opportunity for locals to allow their inner inmates to run amok in public, flouting – for a few hours at least – the prohibitions and taboos of everyday island life.

Nadur has no formal committee and no rules or regulations to bend or break – anything goes, and the mostly young crowds who flock here annually come as much to drink and dance as to gawp at an orgy of blood, guts and gore, with each year's display more demented than the last.

Forget the seductive rustle of peacock feathers or the mystery of masked ballroom dancers. Here you'll find revellers exploring the dark side in more dramatic fashion: some in conventional Halloween spook suits, others emulating members of the clergy or political figures; some dressed as doctors or nurses midway through grisly operations, others simulating sex on floats mocked up to resemble rotating beds.

It's a spectacle as loud as it is lurid, the procession winding its way through town to a symphony of tooting horns, blaring bands and anything else that can add to this most gruesome of gatherings. When it's all said and done, however, the streets empty and the freakishness gets bottled up for another year, and anyone visiting Nadur would have trouble believing that it's anything but the most peaceful of provincial island towns.

Itineraries

National War Museum p38

Malta at War

The ruinous reminders of the devastation unleashed on Malta in World War II are thickest in Valletta, and this day-long tour of its sights gives some indication of how profoundly the island was affected by the conflict.

The country suffered the single heaviest aerial bombardment of any nation in the war – something that earned all of its citizens an unprecedented collective George Cross, now emblazoned on the national flag – and a sense of subdued glory is tangible even on the outskirts of Valletta, where our tour begins, thanks to the **RAF Memorial** (junction of Triq Nelson and Triq Sarria, Floriana), presiding over the bus station beyond the city walls and consisting of a high column topped

by a gilded eagle, wings raised and body poised as if for flight. Yet turn around and you'll find yourself facing a less heroic legacy of the war: the looming **City Gate**, which, along with the area directly behind it, was utterly destroyed by aerial bombardment. Rebuilding was swift and aesthetically rather inconsiderate: the modern City Gate is boxy and visually insipid, the arcades that ring **Freedom Square** beyond it bland and uninspiring. A more accurate depiction of the carnage can, however, be found in Freedom Square itself, where the old **Opera House** – a neo-classical pile built during British rule – still stands exactly as it did following the bombing. Or rather, doesn't stand: the edifice's shattered foundations

Siege Bell Memorial

are all that remain, with the current government joining many of its predecessors in procrastination as to what should take its place.

East of Freedom Square, outside the main gate of Upper Barakka Gardens, signs lead through dim tunnels bored into the Maltese bedrock to the subterranean **Lascaris War Rooms** (p53), from where British forces directed the Mediterranean war effort. The bunker has been recreated as an excellent museum that uses life-size figures and a host of authentic props, maps and period artefacts to show how each room functioned as a dedicated area of operations – from air and coastal defence to mine clearance. Secrecy was of the utmost importance – employees had access to the room in which they worked and no other – and conditions were claustrophobic to say the least. Yet it was from Lascaris that the Allies changed

the course of the war in the Mediterranean, guiding Malta-based submarines to disrupt Axis supplies to North Africa before turning their attention to the invasion of Sicily in Operation Husky, also planned and piloted from Lascaris and the subject of a display in the largest of the museum's chambers.

Follow your trip to the war rooms with a cheap and cheerful lunch stop at the decidedly less claustrophobic **Café Barrakka** (p57), right around the corner in Castille Place, before heading northeast on Triq Sant Ursula. Take a right on Triq San Nikola and you'll find yourself facing Lower Barrakka Gardens and, just beyond them, the seaward-facing **Siege Bell Memorial**, an enormous bell mounted in a stone podium erected in 1992 to mark the 50th anniversary of the end of the war. The bell commemorates the

ITINERARIES

7,000 people – servicemen as well as civilians – who died in Malta during the war, and its toll rings out through the narrow streets of Valletta every day at noon.

From the memorial, press north along Triq Il-Mediterran, following the road as it skirts around Fort St Elmo to the **National War Museum** (p55), which offers a unique collection of military memorabilia, including soldiers' journals and period photographs showing the ravages of aerial bombardment in Malta, as well as armaments from machineguns to anti-aircraft cannons. There's also a captured Italian E-boat, one of six bomb-laden suicide speedboats responsible for an attempt to breach the Grand Harbour that failed when the first two became ensnared in an underwater wire mesh, exploding and bringing down a large bridge (an odd gap in the breakwater, visible from the Siege Bell Memorial, shows where the ruins still lie). Yet the highlight of the museum is *Faith*, one of three Gloucester Gladiator biplanes (the other were called *Hope* and *Charity*) that constituted the entire Maltese air force when the war broke out, and which performed so bravely that the Italian authorities first estimated that they were dealing with at least 25 planes.

The museum is also home to a replica of the nation's collective George Cross medal and the letter that accompanied it, an award bestowed at a point when the German bombardment of Malta was so fierce and relentless that the entire nation was on the brink of starvation. And yet, despite the intensity of the blitz, casualties were kept relatively low thanks to a complex system of underground bunkers in which every one of the islands' inhabitants could be accommodated at any one time.

Four such former shelters are now open as tourist attractions. The best of them, the **Malta At War Museum** (p87), can be found in a courtyard behind the gates of Vittoriosa (a short journey on the no.4 bus from Valletta station, assuming you still have time). The shelter was pickaxed into the bedrock beneath the fortifications, and was large enough to accommodate every man, woman and child living in Vittoriosa, who cowered down here for weeks on end while the German dive-bombers launched one sortie after another in a battle effort to destroy the British Navy ships and dockyard. There was a clinic, a chapel and even classrooms in the shelter – all of which have been recreated with props and original artefacts – while the rest of it consisted of meandering tunnels linking small, cell-like rooms. Each room belonged to a different family, with wooden bunkbeds for sleeping and stone hearths for cooking, and while light was provided with candles, these had to be used sparingly as they depleted the oxygen in the air. Disease was as all-pervading as the constant darkness, and it was a miserable existence, as evinced by several displays in a separate exhibition, one part of which is dedicated to illustrating the immense difficulties overcome in digging the shelter in the first place.

Assuming you still have an appetite after so much death and destruction, finish the tour with a walk down to Vittoriosa Waterfront and a suitably bloodless bite in Malta's only dedicated vegetarian eaterie, the lovely **Tate Café Bar**, or in one of a pair of pricier alternatives, the casino-sited **Ristorante Venezia** or the more enigmatic newcomer **Two and a Half Lemon** (all p90).

St Agatha's Catacombs p40

What Lies Beneath

Having emerged as Malta's first urban settlements more than 2,000 years ago, the ancient capital Mdina and its outlying suburb of Rabat are rich in historical sights – but not all of them can be seen from the surface.

This walking tour of the area's subterranean wonders starts late in the morning and ends in early afternoon (including a break for lunch). It begins at the chilling **Mdina Dungeons** (p106). These chambers served as a prison in medieval times, and today house a permanent exhibition detailing the history of torture in Malta. It's especially unsettling when one realises that certain of the methods depicted took place on this very spot. Among the most unpleasant techniques you'll find examined is the grisly Roman affection for hacking off prisoners' limbs in the most painful and protracted way

possible, with one display outlining how St Agatha had her breasts cut off after allegedly spurning the sexual advances of a Roman governor in Sicily.

Leave the dungeons and walk roughly 100 (330 feet) metres down Triq Villegaignon to Mdina's second underground attraction, a medieval cemetery tucked away beneath the **Carmelite Church** (open 6-10am daily, admission free). The cemetery is dominated by a simple crypt and a statue of the crucifixion, with a seemingly random clutter of graves filling the rest of the available space – some mounted on stone pedestals, others dug into the ground of the crypt itself, and with various flickering candles and marble epitaphs. After the horrors of Mdina Dungeons, this haunting hypogeum is an oasis of tranquility – a place where the clamorous

St Paul's Catacombs

clicks of tourists' cameras become distant memories, and where it's easy to imagine that you've stepped back into medieval times.

The necropolises in next door Rabat, meanwhile, take visitors even further back in time, to the years when Christianity was outlawed, and the ritual burials of its adepts took place in secret catacombs. To get to Rabat, walk out of the Greek Gate in Mdina and down Triq San Pawl to the town centre, stopping – should the inclination take you – for lunch in the lovely **Ristorante Cosmana Navarra** (p108). Suitably recharged and ready for another descent into darkness, you'll find access to the catacombs on Triq Sant Agata. **St Agatha's Catacombs** (p107) is the largest subterranean complex on the islands, in constant use from AD 400 until the 17th century and comprised of two separate chapels. The largest of these features

a standalone stone altar and walls decorated with elaborate frescoes – the earliest are Byzantine images of the Madonna and St Paul, while later additions depict St Agatha, the saint who spent many months hiding from the Romans within these very chambers. Part of the complex is open to the public and comprises a maze of tunnels flanked by open sarcophagi – some of them still housing partly decayed skeletons – which finally terminates at a primitive crypt featuring a frescoed altarpiece rich in religious symbolism (the shell represents heaven, the pigeon is the soul and the tree a metaphor for the earthly life).

Exiting on to the same street, double back towards the town square and you'll eventually come to **St Paul's Catacombs** (p107). Dating back to somewhere between AD 500 and 600, these catacombs are stylistically very different from St Agatha's: smaller and more claustrophobic, and with virtually every square metre utilised to house its roughly 1,000 separate sarcophagi. The front section is home to a primitive chapel where mourners congregated during ritualistic burials, from which point emanate haphazard tunnels cluttered with countless tombs – from small recesses cut into the walls and generally used to inter babies and children (*loculi*) and larger graves dug directly into the ground (*arcosolium*) to canopied tombs set on elaborate stone pedestals high above the floor.

A short walk from the catacombs is Rabat's town square, a bustling space dominated by **St Paul's Cathedral** (p107) and with a couple of old-fashioned cafés popular with elderly men, many of whom while away lazy afternoons with their pet greenfinches trilling in portable cages. Beneath the surface, however, it's a different story altogether, with two separate subterranean spaces including a natural cave under the cathedral itself known as **St Paul's Grotto** (p108). While waiting to stand trial in Rome for heresy (a charge for which he was eventually beheaded), St Paul is believed to have spent three months in AD 60 giving sermons and performing baptisms in this cave, and is therefore credited with having introduced Christianity to Malta. The cave itself has been a place of devout pilgrimage ever since, although there's little to see, the small and musty space largely empty save for a statue of the saint, a silver model of a galley and four lamps contributed by Pope Paul VI.

Across the street, the square's other underground attraction is an **air raid shelter** excavated in World War II to shield locals from bombardment. Such installations were dug all over the island, and Rabat's is typical of the general design employed: a network of arterial tunnels branching out from a main central tunnel and lined with tiny cell-like rooms – some of which served as makeshift clinics, classrooms and chapels, but most of them built to accommodate the local populace. Rooms were allocated on a means-tested basis – the wealthier the family, the bigger the cell – but no amount of money could offset the squalor, with a combination of stale air, damp and warmth providing the perfect conditions for diseases to flourish. The shelter, beneath the current **Wignacourt Museum** (p108), is largely unembellished these days, so you'll be forced to use your imagination to conjure up its wartime incarnation.

Rabat's last underground sight is (mercifully) much less steeped in misery, and can be found inside the looming **Dominican Monastery** at the south-easterly end of Triq Il-Kullegg. The monastery (open 9am-7pm daily, admission free), which dates from 1462, is the site of an underground cave where – so the story goes – a local hunter taking shelter from the rain was once visited by a vision of the Madonna, after which the cave became a site of pilgrimage. The Dominicans later arrived from Sicily to set up a branch in Malta and chose to build their monastery on top of the venerated cave, which they turned into a chapel: it's now a chamber rich with ornamentation, with marbled walls and a central altar featuring an elaborate fresco of the Madonna ascending towards heaven. The fame of the chapel has long since faded – its flock now comprises a few elderly women who come to mumble the rosary – but it still warrants a visit on any tour of Malta's intriguing subterranean cities.

ITINERARIES

San Anton Palace & Gardens p44

The Three Villages

Located in the centre of Malta, the historic settlements of Lija, Balzan and Attard are known collectively as the Three Villages, although their streets merge so seamlessly that casual visitors will find it hard to tell where one ends and the next begins. Not that this should dissuade them from visiting: the charming Baroque architecture and myriad churches and chapels lining the villages' narrow streets offer glimpses of a Malta that's fast disappearing under the speculative eye of the property developer.

A tour of the villages can easily be drawn out to take up the better part of a day. Begin your walk in **Lija** on Vjal It-Trasfigurazzjoni, where you'll find the four-tiered **Lija Tower** (affectionately known to locals as the 'Wedding Cake'). This elaborate folly once stood in the grand garden of Villa Depiro Gougion, now Gallery G, and was

originally built for the villa's owner, Marquis Depiro. Looming large behind the Wedding Cake is Lija's **Church of St Saviour**, an imposing place of worship designed by a local architect for the Order of St John, one Giovanni Barbara, who laid the first stone in 1694. Its Baroque façade has two bell towers and two clock faces – one real, one painted – while the austere interior boasts a typically Maltese marble patterned floor, a large dome and several altars. Less traditional is its stained-glass window, dating from 1903 and once again bright and beaming despite spending World War II buried in a grave beneath the chapel for safety.

The church and the village both come to life on Lija's **Feast of the Transfiguration** on 6 August, when the church is decked out with a wealth of gold and silver items and relics usually locked away in

ITINERARIES

its treasury. Most impressive given the full glare of the intense summer sun is the sight of ten grown men sweating beneath the weight of the church's enormous statue of Jesus, Moses and Elijah, which they heave around the village streets for more than three hours (it takes 18 men to get the statue through the church door). The statue was created by Carlo Darmanin in 1864, although the gilded wooden base has been worn out and replaced several times since, with all previous incarnations sent to the local bakery at the end of their lives and symbolically burned on the stove (Triq Il-Forn or 'Old Bakery Street' lies directly behind the church).

With the church in front of you, turn right and walk a few metres along Triq Sir Ugo Mifsud to the bright blue shuttered **Gallery G** (no.4, 2142 1984), the striking original façade of which remains despite developers having snapped up much of the garden over the years. The gallery itself showcases the work of mostly local artists.

From the gallery, return to the church and continue along the same road until its name changes to Triq Il-Kbira ('Main Street'). This is a typical Lija street, narrow and peaceful and with countless colourful doorways all opening directly on to the road. Whatever the weather, arrive early enough and you'll find dozens of locals of all ages rushing down the street to morning mass; arrive a little later and you might catch them returning to find that the baker has left a *hobza* (Maltese loaf) tied to their door knob in a knotted carrier bag. Forge onwards to where Il-Kbira veers left and you'll find the **Chapel of Santa Maria** (open 8am-8pm daily), worth a peek for its highly decorative interior.

Continue along Il-Kbira until you reach a crossroads and you'll find yourself facing the **Three Villages Bar** (no.150, 2148 7032) – an appropriate moniker given that the building straddles the junction where the three villages meet (the bar itself is located in **Balzan**, though one wall technically falls in Attard and if you're facing it from across the road you're standing in Lija). The bar is run by four sisters and has been in the same family for over a century, nor has much changed in that time beyond the colour of the crisp packets – from the unadorned walls, and dark display cabinets to the dim electric lighting and four square tables.

Suitably revived, and with the bar on your right, walk down the hill along yet another Triq Il-Kbira, this one among the most desirable addresses in Balzan, its houses a picturesque clutter of columns, shutters and traditional Maltese balconies painted in bright primary colours. The street ends at a pretty square, a popular meeting place in temperate weather for elderly gentlemen who while away their twilight years with protracted afternoons of games and gossip. On one side is the 17th-century **Church of the Annunciation**, combining a grand Tuscan exterior with a Doric interior complete with beautiful painted ceilings and elaborate gilding on the raised organ. It's a far more decorative church than Lija's, nor does it like to be outdone in the field of pomp and ceremony: Balzan's own feast day, which falls on the second Sunday in July, sees its statue of Mary and Gabriel, by Salvatore Dimech, raised aloft and carried through the village for hours.

From the sacred to the (mildly) profane, the popular local wine bar **Fra Giuseppe** (3 Triq Dun Spir Sammut, 2149 9940) sits peacefully behind the church and serves fine wines, bar food (including fondues) and a generous helping of local history: built in 1717, the original owner, Joseph Sammut, was a personal doctor to the Knights.

Head across the square along Triq Il-Imejda and take a right

on to Triq Il-Papa Alessandru VII. Cross the main road – Triq Birbal – and continue to the junction of Vjal Il-Bon Pasteur, which in turn brings you to the remains of the **Wignacourt Aqueduct** – built in the 16th century by noted local architect Tumas Dingli to carry water from Rabat to the then burgeoning city of Valletta. Turn back and retrace your steps down Triq Birbal until you reach the third and final village of **Attard**, home to the beautiful **San Anton Palace & Gardens** (p119). The building itself – parts of which are open to the public – is the official presidential residence, but it's the gardens, created in 1882, that constitute the main attraction here: vividly green, teeming with colourful flowers and home to countless arterial pathways and charming ponds. While the somewhat unkempt aviaries are best steered clear of – the local cats and laconic turtles seem to have far more fun than their feathered friends – this rarely crowded space is an otherwise tranquil oasis on

Etienne Locum Vinim

ITINERARIES

an island that seems to have more construction cranes than trees, and the perfect place unwind.

Leave the garden by the same entrance and take a right along Triq Lord Strickland, at the end of which you'll reach Triq San Antnin and a large garden wall belonging to **Villa Bologna** (85 Triq San Antnin, 2141 1111) – a privately owned house built in 1745 by Fabrizio Grech as a dowry for his daughter's wedding. Lord Gerald Strickland, Maltese prime minister between 1927 and 1932, also once resided here. The gardens (extravagantly embellished by Lady Strickland) feature citrus groves, fountains, vine-covered pergolas and ponds, and while closed to the general public, tour groups can view them by appointment. A short walk up from the blue garden gate is the villa's former stables, now home to local pottery **Ceramica Saracine** (87-88 Triq San Antnin, 2144 0979, open 8.30am-5pm Tue, Thur).

Across from Villa Bologna, Triq San Antnin turns into what is easily Attard's most beautiful street, lined with what are best described as miniature stately homes that in turn lead to rows of genteel terraced houses. Keep these houses on your left and walk on to a small roundabout, crossing straight over to access yet another Triq Il-Kbira, which leads past the US ambassador's house to the centre of Attard and its parish **Church of St Mary**, smaller and with considerably less gilding than Balzan's own house of prayer. Triq Il-Kbira is also home to a fantastic local restaurant, **Etienne Locum Vinim** (see p119).

Retrace your steps a little and take a left down Triq Il-Linja, following it until you reach **Santa Lucia** (2166 1755), surely one of the island's best and busiest cafés. It's the perfect place to finish your tour of the Three Villages over a *pastizzi* and a glass of Kinnie (a non-alcoholic Maltese beverage made of bitter oranges and herbs), before turning around and heading back to the Wedding Cake, no more than a 15-minute walk from here.

Airline flights are one of the biggest producers of the global warming gas CO_2. But with **The CarbonNeutral Company** you can make your travel a little greener.

Go to **www.carbonneutral.com** to calculate your flight emissions then 'neutralise' them through international projects which save exactly the same amount of carbon dioxide.

Contact us at **shop@carbonneutral.com** or call into the office on **0870 199 99 88** for more details.

CarbonNeutral®flights

Malta by Area

Grand Harbour

Valletta

A designated World Heritage Site spanning less than two kilometres (1.25 miles) at its longest point, Valletta – founded by the Knights of St John following their victory in the Great Seige of 1565 – is home to some of Malta's finest historical attractions.

The city's major sights are found around the main thoroughfare, pedestrianised Republic Street, which runs the length of Valletta from City Gate to **Fort St Elmo**, the latter famous for the frontline role it played in both the Great Siege of 1565 and in World War II. Republic Street's biggest crowd-puller is the Knights' own **St John's Co-Cathedral**, erected in the 1570s and one of the most ornate Baroque churches in the world, while other sights include the excellent **National Museum of Archaeology** and the **National Library**, the last public building erected by the Knights before they ceded Malta to Napoleon. Adjoining the library is the majestic **Grand Master's Palace**, Malta's centre of rule since 1571 and home to its Parliament, the State Rooms of which are open to the public.

Valletta is also the site of more than a dozen churches – it's well worth stopping in on the richly Baroque **St Paul's Shipwreck Church** and the unusually spartan **Jesuits Church** – as well as several museums and galleries. Foremost among these are the **National Museum of Fine Arts** and contemporary arts hub the **St James Cavalier Centre for Creativity**. The story of Malta's intense suffering in World War II is told in two museums: the **Lascaris**

War Rooms, the reconstructed subterranean nerve centre for the Maltese war effort, and the **National War Museum**.

Far more peaceful are Valletta's two public gardens, loftily set on the ramparts of the city. Hastings Garden, which has recently been re-landscaped, offers a fine view of Marsamxett Harbour as well as large swathes of Malta. Also recently restored, Upper Barrakka Gardens overlooks the splendid Grand Harbour, with the medieval Three Cities of Senglea, Vittoriosa and Cospicua in the background. Nearby, the intimidating Auberge de Castille encloses the Prime Minister's Office in a glorious exterior set with triumphal symbols and columns.

Directly beneath Upper Barrakka Gardens, Valletta Waterfront is lined with restored Pinto Stores, many of which these days house restaurants and bars with sweeping views of historic Fort St Angelo's magnificent rise from the waters of the Grand Harbour.

Sights & museums

Casa Rocca Piccola

74 Republic Street (2122 1499/ www.casaroccapiccola.com). **Open** 10am-4pm Mon-Sat. **Admission** €5.82. **Map** p51 D3 ❶

This palace, built by an Italian knight in 1580, is now a museum of artefacts providing an insight into Maltese nobility over the centuries – from the private chapel to the wood-panelled living room complete with ivory chess set and historic paintings. The garden of citrus trees is a real rarity – gardens were long ago outlawed in Valletta to make best use of the limited space. Tours take place on the hour.

Fort St Elmo

St Elmo Street (2123 7747/www.visit malta.com). **Open** Re-enactments 11am Sun (late Sept-early July). **Admission** free. **Map** p51 F3 ❷

Upper Barrakka Gardens

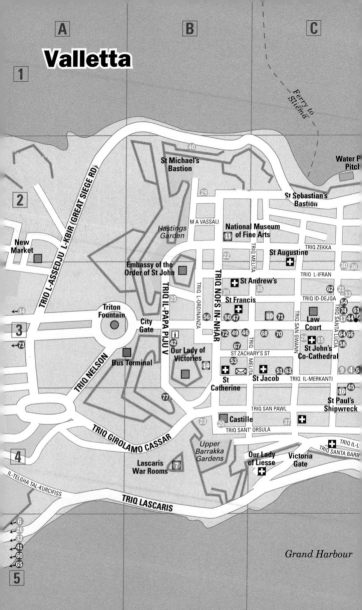

Valletta

A B C

1

2

3

4

5

St Michael's Bastion

St Sebastian's Bastion

Water P Pitch

Ferry to Sliema

40

29

M A VASSALI

National Museum of Fine Arts

11

22

St Augustine

TRIQ ZEKKA

TRIQ MELITA

TRIQ L-IFRAN

30 36

New Market

Hastings Garden

Embassy of the Order of St John

St Andrew's

39

35

St Francis

62

21 21

54

TRIQ ID-DEJQA

TRIQ SANTA LUCIA

59

17 74

44

TRIQ NOFS IN-NHAR

TRIQ L-ORDINANZA

25

56

50

47

10 71

Law Court

64 66

58

TRIQ L-ASSEDJU L-KBIR (GREAT SIEGE RD)

TRIQ IL-PAPA PIJU V

TRIQ IN

Triton Fountain

City Gate

42

Our Lady of Victories

72

49

46

67

68

70

TRIQ SAN GWANN

28

St John's Co-Cathedral

9 45

← 34

← 73

14

ST ZACHARY'S ST

53

St Catherine

51 63

St Jacob

MELITA

TRIQ IL-MERKANTI

Bus Terminal

TRIQ NELSON

77

16 45

St Paul's Shipwreck

23

Castille

20

37

TRIQ SAN PAWL

TRIQ SANT' ORSULA

TRIQ GIROLAMO CASSAR

Upper Barrakka Gardens

Our Lady of Liesse

Victoria Gate

TRIQ IL-L

TRIQ SANTA BARB

Lascaris War Rooms

7

IL-TELGHA TAL-KURCIFISS

TRIQ LASCARIS

Grand Harbour

← 6
← 29
← 32
← 41
← 60
← 65

D   **E**   **F**

0   200 m

0   200 yds

© Copyright Time Out Group 2008

1

Marsamxett Harbour

2

St Sebastian's
Bastion

XQ MARSAMXETT

St Paul's
Cathedral

Auberge
d'Aragon

TRIQ IL-PUNENT

Archbishop's
Palace

Our Lady of
Mount Carmel

Manoel
Theatre

French Curtain

St Gregory's
Bastion

St Gregory's
Curtain

Ball's
Bastion

National
War Museum

TRIQ SAN BASTJAN

English Curtain

TRIQ SAN KRISTOFRU

TRIQ L-ARCISOOF

TRIQ SAN GUZEPP

TRIQ IT-TRAMUNTANA

TRIQ L-INFERMERJA

TRIQ SAN NIKOLA

38

3

TRIQ IR-REPUBBLIKA

19

1

Fort St Elmo

2

8

Abercrombie's
Bastion

i

SAN FREDERICK

Grand Master's
Palace &
Armoury

Greek
Catholic

St Dominic

Fort St Elmo
Museum

Abercrombie's
Curtain

*St Elmo
Point*

TRIQ IL-MERKANTI

Mediterranean
Conference
Centre

76

Jesuits Church

5

TRIQ SAN PAWL

TRIQ SAN DUMINKU

TRIQ MEDITERRAN

St Lazarus
Bastion

TRIQ SANT' ORSULA

27

St Ursula

TRIQ IL-MEDITERRAN

St Lazarus
Curtain

4

X-XATT IL-BARRIERA

Fish Market

Siege Bell Memorial

5

Built in 1552, Malta's most famous fort took the Ottoman Turks one month to breach during the Great Siege of 1565 – a fact attributed to its controversial star-shaped construction. St Elmo also played a dramatic role in World War II, when it took the first of countless bombs dropped on Malta. Today it houses a police academy and is open most Sundays for colourful military re-enactments and pageantry parades.

Grand Master's Palace & Armoury

Merchants Street (2124 9349/www. heritagemalta.org). **Open** *State Rooms* 10am-4pm Mon-Wed, Fri-Sun. Closed during state visits. *Palace Armoury* 9am-5pm daily. **Admission** *State Rooms & Palace Armoury* €4.66; €1.16-€2.33 reductions. **Map** p51 D3 ❸

The Grand Master's Palace has been Malta's seat of power since its foundation in 1571. The five State Rooms feature coffered timber ceilings, priceless furniture, plus paintings of knightly pomp and British royals (most of them installed during British rule); there are also frescoes and paintings in the wide corridors, many depicting naval battles and romantic Maltese scenes, while the coats of arms of the Grand Masters are displayed on the floors in inlaid marble. The Knights' past glory is further evidenced in the magnificent Armoury, which houses more than 5,000 pieces of military hardware, with the gilded parade armour of various old Grand Masters taking pride of place.

The Great Siege of Malta & the Knights of St John

Café Premier Complex, Republic Square, Republic Street (2124 7300/www.great siege.com.mt). **Open** 10am-4pm daily. **Admission** €8.15; €6.41 reductions. **Map** p50 C3 ❹

This audio-visual show uses video clips, theatrical wax dummies and computer-generated visuals to tell the story of the Knights of Malta from their foundation to their departure in 1798. The 45-minute walk-through allows

Grand Master's Palace & Armoury

MALTA BY AREA

visitors to absorb the story of the Knights as it unfolds in the meandering hallways and rooms – a basic introduction at best, but great fun for kids.

Jesuits Church

Archbishop Street (no phone). **Open** 6am-12.30pm Mon-Fri, Sun; 6am-12.30pm, 5-8pm Sat. **Admission** free. **Map** p51 D4 ⑤

Rebuilt in 1634 with an elaborate Baroque façade, the Jesuits Church is situated within the grounds of the old University of Malta, itself established by the Jesuits. It has a simple whitewashed interior with a raised podium above the altar, and the St Paul's Street side of the building boasts one of Malta's oldest sundials.

The Knights Spectacular 1565

Powerhouse Theatre, Valletta Waterfront (9999 1565/www.malta 1565.com). **Open** *Shows* 8.30pm Thur (additional days in summer, phone for details). **Admission** €34.94; €16.31 reductions. **Map** p50 A5 ⑥

This action-packed spectacle recounts the Great Siege of 1565 with a 50-strong cast, nine beautiful horses, dancing girls, an able falconer and valiant Knights in shining armour. The narrator Melita guides visitors through a tale that is both informative and entertaining, with the atmosphere swinging from festive to fearful as the Turks attack and the Knights fight on. Children will almost certainly be enthralled for the duration.

Lascaris War Rooms

The Ditch (2123 4936). **Open** 9.30am-4pm Mon-Fri; 9.30am-12.30pm Sat, Sun. **Admission** €4.08; €1.98 reductions. **Map** p50 B4 ⑦

In dungeons deep beneath the Valletta bedrock – originally excavated by the Knights as prison cells for their slaves – the World War II era is reconstructed in the very same rooms that the British forces planned the war effort in Malta, plotting the submarine attacks that disrupted Axis supplies. Wartime props and waxworks add plenty of character

Short fuses

Malta's fireworks scare more than just the pets.

Fireworks are proving a big headache for the Maltese authorities – and it's not just the noise. The national pyrotechnics industry is largely the work of dozens of semi-legal 'factories' that are often little more than ramshackle sheds, and as celebratory feast days approach such buildings will be packed with explosives that can and do go off without warning.

In 2007 alone there were eight deaths caused by explosions at fireworks factories. The national Pyrotechnics Commission is perpetually drawing up laws to reduce to danger (including one, frequently flouted, that demands a 183-metre/600-foot buffer zone between factories and the nearest road, office or residence), but those making the fireworks often do so as a hobby more than a livelihood, and are determined to carry on regardless of the laws.

As such, Malta's summer feast days continue to provide some of the most kaleidoscopic displays around. Lija's **Feast of the Transfiguration** (6 August, also p42) is one of the best by far, while the **Feast of the Assumption** (15 August) and **Victory Day** (8 September) are celebrated in villages and towns across the islands. Also well worth catching are the **National Mechanical Ground Fireworks Festival** in April and the **Malta International Fireworks Festival** in May (locations vary for both).

For more on Malta's feast days and festivals, see pp30-34.

MALTA BY AREA

De Robertis
Roof Top Restaurant

*Serving A La Carte, Menu Du Jour
and a Mediterranean Cuisine Menu,
the De Robertis Roof Top Restaurant is situated on
the highest point in Valletta, overlooking the Grand Harbour,
the Three Cities and the magnificent fortifications
lit up at night. Entrance is through Castille Hotel.
Ample parking space.*

Castille Hotel ❖

*Castille Square, Valletta, Malta.
Tel: 21243678, 21220173 Fax: 21243679
info@hotelcastillemalta.com
www.hotelcastillemalta.com*

(near Upper Barrakka Gardens)

to proceedings, while an informative audio commentary recounts the dramatic details of the various operations that went on in each room.

The Malta Experience

St Elmo Bastions, Mediterranean Street (2124 3776/www.themalta experience.com). **Open** *Shows* on the hr 11am-4pm Mon-Fri; 11am-1pm Sat, Sun, public hols. Also 2pm Sat Oct-June. **Admission** €8.15; €4.08-€5.82 reductions. **Map** p51 F3 ❽

This well-produced documentary offers interesting and often beautiful footage of Maltese landscapes and covers the various historical eras with entertaining verve – although it's fair to say that summarising 7,000 years of Maltese development in a one-hour film offers only a rudimentary introduction to the history of the island.

National Library

36 Old Treasury Street (2123 6585). **Open** *mid June-Sept* 8.15am-1pm Mon-Sat. *Oct-mid June* 8.15am-12.15pm, 1.30-5pm Mon-Fri; 8.15am-1pm Sat. **Admission** free. **Map** p50 C3 ❾

The National Library was the last public building erected by the Knights in the 1790s and was designed as a marriage of Baroque and neo-classical styles. It now holds Malta's official historical archives, including all state archives of the Knights from their formation in 1113 to the end of their rule in Malta in 1798. The main reading hall alone contains 40,000 books stacked from floor to ceiling, with important national documents and historical Maltese currency displayed in charmingly old-fashioned glass cases.

National Museum of Archaeology

Auberge de Provence, Republic Street (2122 1623/www.heritagemalta.org). **Open** 9am-5pm daily. **Admission** €2.33; €0.58-€1.16 reductions. **Map** p50 C3 ❿

Malta's incredible Neolithic relics are here displayed chronologically from 5200 to 2500 BC. The pottery bowls and funereal furnishings of the earliest Neolithic settlers are simple, but the exhibits of the next hall – including a large stone pot and stone-carved spiral motifs unearthed in the Neolithic Temple of Tarxien – are resonant with symbolic meaning and illustrate the rapid creative evolution of Malta's Neolithic community. The zenith of Neolithic art is displayed in the fascinating collection of human figures, ranging from arcane stone heads and small statuettes to full-size representations of the deity referred to as the 'Fat Lady', the focus of what is believed to have been an ancient fertility cult. The last of the museum's rooms exhibits pottery, tools, beads and many other ornaments. The museum is itself located within the extremely well-preserved Auberge de Provence, the richly painted walls and wooden beamed ceilings of which make it one of the finest buildings in Valletta.

National Museum of Fine Arts

South Street (2122 5769/www. heritagemalta.org). **Open** 9am-5pm daily. **Admission** €2.33; €0.58-€1.16 reductions. **Map** p50 B2 ⓫

Housed in a lavish rococo palace, this revered national treasure trove of art begins in the 14th century and groups paintings together by schools. The best works are by the Italian Baroque artist Mattia Preti, whose intense biblical depictions occupy two rooms, and by France's Antoine de Favray, whose portraits of the Knights take up another room. There is also a good selection of paintings by Malta's most famous artist Giuseppe Cali, as well as a great deal of glittering Maltese silverware. Much of the collection was originally displayed in buildings of the Order of St John before being administered by the State following the Knights' departure in 1798.

National War Museum

Fort St Elmo (2122 2430/www. heritagemalta.org). **Open** 9am-5pm daily. **Admission** €2.33; €0.58-€1.16 reductions. **Map** p51 E3 ⓬

MALTA BY AREA

The National War Museum houses a large display of World War II memorabilia and offers an absorbing insight into Malta's important military role in the post-1800 era under British rule. Among the exhibits are guns, jeeps, aircraft and the remains of an Italian U-boat, one of many laden with bombs and rammed into Maltese targets during suicide missions. There is also a very moving collection of photographs depicting the difficult conditions suffered by the Maltese from 1940 to 1943, plus an array of military uniforms, badges, medals, soldiers' diaries and a replica of the George Cross awarded to the Maltese nation for bravery and endurance in the face of near-starvation and blanket aerial bombardment.

Our Lady of Mount Carmel

Old Theatre Street (no phone). **Open** 7am-7pm daily. **Admission** free. **Map** p51 D2 ⑬

One of Valletta's largest churches, the enigmatic egg-shaped dome of Our Lady of Mount Carmel was completed in the 1980s and can be seen for miles around. The church is built over an original chapel erected in 1573 and destroyed during World War II. There's little in the way of outstanding artistic detail, but it's worth a peep for sheer scale alone: the interior is cavernous and the dome dizzyingly high.

Our Lady of Victory

Victory Square (no phone). **Open** 7.30am-10am Mon, Wed-Fri; 7.30am-noon Tue; 7.30am-10am, 6-8pm Sat. **Admission** free. **Map** p50 B3 ⑭

Built to commemorate the Knights' victory over the Ottomans in the Great Siege of 1565 – hence its name – tradition holds that the foundation stone of the city of Valletta was laid on this spot by Grand Master La Valette in 1566. This thus served as the first of the Order's churches in Valletta until 1577, when the Conventual Church of St John was completed. Grand Master La Valette was himself originally buried here before his remains were transferred to the Co-Cathedral.

St John's Co-Cathedral

St John's Street (2122 0536). **Open** 9.30am-4.30pm Mon-Fri; 9.30am-12.30pm Sat. **Admission** €5.82; free-€1.98 reductions. **Map** p50 C3 ⑮

Designed by Maltese architect Girolmu Cassar and completed in the 1570s to serve as the Knights' conventual place of worship, St John's Co-Cathedral is one of the most opulent churches in the world. The original exterior remains untouched, but as the threat of war receded in the 17th century the Knights engaged the Italian Baroque artist Mattia Preti to supervise the artistic re-creation of the Co-Cathedral's interior. It took Preti five years to paint the 18 vignettes on the vault depicting episodes from the life of St John the Baptist; in later years he also painted the altarpieces of the nine side chapels. Preti also sculpted the Oratory – a place of worship for novice Knights – to house Caravaggio's *The Beheading of St John the Baptist*, painted in 1608 during the artist's brief stint in Malta after fleeing Italy as a man wanted for murdering his opponent in a duel.

Some of the moveable riches that adorned the church in its heyday are now exhibited in a museum adjoining the building: these include silverware, vestments, illuminated choral books, portraits of Knights and, most valuable, three sets of tapestries quilted in 1702 by the Flemish artist Jodicos de Vos and depicting various religious episodes and characters.

St Paul's Shipwreck Church

St Paul Street (2123 6013). **Open** 6.30am-7pm daily. **Admission** free. **Map** p50 C4 ⑯

Dedicated to the shipwreck of St Paul in Malta in AD 60, this church has been remodelled three times since its original construction in 1571. Many of the treasures housed within its ornate, marble-clad interior date from the church's earliest history, with many more added throughout the centuries: some of the most notable works include the altarpiece by Italian artist Matteo

Auberge de Castille p49

MALTA BY AREA

D'Aleccio, the paintings of Attilio Palombi and Giuseppe Cali, and Lorenzo Gafa's looming dome. The church is also home to a fragment of St Paul's wristbone set in an ornate gold reliquary and part of the column to which he was reputedly tied during his beheading in Rome.

The Wartime Experience

Embassy Complex, Santa Lucia Street (2122 2225/www.embassycomplex. com.mt). **Open** *Shows* on the hr 10am-1pm daily. **Admission** €5.12; €3.49 reductions. **Map** p50 C3 ⑰

Those seeking an insight into how the entire Maltese nation ended up receiving a collective St George's Cross would do well to visit the Wartime Experience, a 45-minute documentary focusing on the savage bombardment of the island during World War II and the gallantry of its inhabitants.

Eating & drinking

Ambrosia

137 Archbishop Street (2122 5923). **Open** 12.30-2pm, 7.30-10pm Mon-Sat. Closed 2wks Aug. **€€**. **French**. **Map** p51 D3 ⑱

Ambrosia's inventive menu satisfies a faithful clientele with consistently good French dishes. Starters include asparagus with walnuts and ricotta salata, tender calves' liver or pumpkin soup drizzled with truffle oil; mains offer delicious dorado when in season, beef braised in wine, and lamb shanks. Chocolate pudding served with crème anglaise heads up a decent dessert menu, while warm yellow walls and antique chairs add a touch of class.

Blue Room

59 Republic Street (2123 8014). **Open** noon-3pm, 7-11pm daily. **€€**. **Chinese**. **Map** p51 D3 ⑲

A popular Chinese restaurant with an interesting mix of oriental and contemporary decor – the ultra-modern chandelier hanging proudly in the middle of the main room is a real eye-catcher. Specialities include aromatic duck served with pancakes, sizzling plates such as fillet of beef and a range of warming curry dishes.

Café Barrakka

Castille Place (2122 3744). **Open** 10am-3pm Tue-Sun; 6-10pm Thur-Sat. **€**. **Maltese**. **Map** p50 B4 ⑳

Café Jubilee

With everything from baked macaroni to beef and turkey roasts for as little as €2.33, this must be the cheapest eaterie in Valletta. Nor is quality sacrificed: €4.66 will buy you a slow-cooked lamb shank in mint and tomato sauce or a superb dish of mushroom or fish ravioli. Weekend evenings bring a truly gut-busting €10.48 buffet.

Café Jubilee
125 Santa Lucia Street (2125 2332/www.cafejubilee.com). **Open** 8am-1am daily. **Café**. **Map** p50 C3 ㉑
A cosy if occasionally crowded venue decorated with a wallpaper of vintage newspapers and a kaleidoscope of curio prints. Affordable, informal meals range from pea or ricotta pastries and pies to soups and traditional Italian pasta dishes: try the own-made ravioli filled with Gozo cheese and served with a butter and sage or cream, pine nut and sun-dried tomato sauce.

Carriage
22 Valletta Buildings, South Street (2124 7828). **Open** noon-3.30pm Mon-Thur; noon-3.30pm, 7.30-11pm Fri; 7.30-11pm Sat. Closed 2wks Aug. €€€. **French**. **Map** p50 B2 ㉒

Entrance to the Carriage is through an office block and via a lift – ask for a window seat and soak up the extensive vista of city rooftops and the surrounding sea. Light and creatively modern French dishes are the order of the day – from own-made ravioli and fresh mushrooms filled with prawns and ginger for starters, to braised saddle of rabbit and stuffed quail for mains.

Castille Wine Vaults
Castille Place (2123 7707). **Open** 7pm-1am Tue-Sun. Closed Aug. **Bar**. **Map** p50 B4 ㉓
Housed in a vaulted cellar built by the Knights as an underground arms cache, Malta's largest wine bar serves local and foreign vintages to knowing connoisseurs and complete newcomers alike. Busy on winter weekends, quieter in summers, it accompanies wines by the bottle or glass with snacks including platters of cheeses, cured meats or seafood (€5.82).

Fumia
Old Bakery Street (2131 7053). **Open** *Restaurant* 12.30-2.30pm, 7.30-10.30pm Tue-Sun. *Café* 8.30am-8.30pm Tue-Sun. €€€. **Italian**. **Map** p51 D3 ㉔

MALTA BY AREA

Located in an impeccably restored cellar directly beneath the Manoel Theatre, Fumia serves the best and freshest fish around (meat doesn't even feature on the menu), either steamed or *al sale* (roasted in a crust of sea salt). Superb pasta dishes include fresh ravioli stuffed with ricotta and squid ink or salmon and creamed shrimp, while the cannoli and cassatella siciliana head up a range of hearty desserts.

Fusion Four

1 St John's Cavalier Street (2122 5255). **Open** 7.30pm-1am Tue, Sat, Sun; noon-3pm, 7.30pm-1am Wed-Fri. **€€**. **Fusion**. **Map** p50 B3 ㉕

Tricky to find but well worth the search, Fusion Four dazzles with daring dishes from chicken breast in a chilli and mango sauce to fish cooked with a pistachio crust. Desserts, including both a white chocolate mousse and sublime banoffee pie, are also to die for. The restaurant is located in the former stables of the nearby Cavalier of St John and boasts a lovely alfresco terrace tucked between the bastions.

Hard Rock Café

Valletta Waterfront (2123 3346). **Open** 10am-11.30pm daily. **Bar**. **Map** p50 A5 ㉖

Indoors it's your typical Hard Rock Café, with branded clothes and tourist-friendly accessories for sale, although this Waterfront building has retained the features of the original Knights-built store in which it's housed. Those about to rock will find a list of 31 colourful cocktails to help them do so.

Il-Horza

NEW *6 St Christopher's Street (2122 6936).* **Open** noon-3pm Mon-Wed, Sun; noon-3pm, 7-10.30pm Thur-Sat. **€€**. **Mediterranean**. **Map** p51 D4 ㉗

This small and unassuming restaurant is hugely popular with the capital's professionals at lunchtimes. With no set menu and dishes changing daily depending on ingredients available, Il-Horza serves mostly meat and fish dishes, with notable highlights including Chianina steak from Florence and an unusual prickly pear crumble, plus around 90 different wines.

Kantina Café & Wine Bar p61

MALTA BY AREA

Kantina Café & Wine Bar

103 St John's Street (2123 0096).
Open *Jan-Apr* 8am-8pm Mon-Sat.
May-Dec 8am-midnight Mon-Sat.
Café. Map p50 C3 ㉘
With outdoor tables in the shade of the
large trees by St John's Co-Cathedral,
this must be one of the capital's prettiest spots for a light snack or afternoon
tipple. There are fresh salads and great
sandwiches mixing seasonal and
regional ingredients (the tuna, olive
and peppery *ghejna* cheese sandwich
is fantastic), plus the opportunity to
create your own plate from a large variety of fresh vegetables and cold cuts
under the counter.

Lantern

20 Sappers Street (2123 7521). **Open**
11.30am-3pm, 6.30-11pm Mon-Sat.
€€. **Mediterranean**. Map p50 B2 ㉙
The kitschy baroque decor won't be to
everyone's taste, but food at the
Lantern is excellent and inexpensive.
Fish-lovers opt for the catch of the day,
grilled lightly and served with a choice
of dressings; pasta is also popular, with
a daily special along the lines of macaroni with almonds, cream, green peppers and mushrooms. There's also a set
two-course lunch menu (with a glass of
wine) for a very reasonable €9.90.

Legligin

119 Santa Lucia Street (2122 1699).
Open 7.30-11pm Tue-Thur, Sat, Sun;
noon-11pm Fri. **Mediterranean**. **€€**.
Map p50 C3 ㉚
A charming wine bar and restaurant
near the Manoel Theatre, where owner
Chris Misfud Bonnici and his trusty
two-burner stove concoct tapas-sized
portions of dishes such as pork in
honey, snail stew and rabbit-stuffed
ravioli, all gobbled with gusto in a
cellar-like room seating no more than
20. Just watch out for those winding
stairs if you've been over-indulging in
the formidable wine list.

Malata

Palace Square (2123 3967). **Open**
noon-3pm, 7-11pm Mon-Sat. **€€€**.
French. Map p51 D3 ㉛

Adventurous and creative French cuisine infused with Mediterranean ingredients, served either alfresco in elegant
Palace Square or in a vaulted cellar, its
walls covered with cartoons of Maltese
politicians and with live jazz every
Tuesday and Thursday evening in the
summer months. Mains are along the
lines of linguini with sea urchins, quail
with foie gras, traditionally roasted
rabbit and lightly grilled fish fillets,
while those with a sweet tooth will find
that the crème brûlée is simply not to
be missed. Worth every penny.

Nan Yuan

*Valletta Waterfront (2122 5310/
www.nanyuan.com.mt).* **Open** 11am-
2pm, 7-11pm Tue-Sun. **€€**. **Chinese**.
Map p50 A5 ㉜
Ideally located on spectacular Valletta
Waterfront, Nan Yuan is increasingly
popular thanks to some truly exquisite
Cantonese cuisine, which is both
affordable and served in portions large
enough to satisfy even the hearty
Maltese appetite. Favourites include
sizzling beef, delicate almond chicken
and tender lamb cooked with ginger
and herbs, and all dishes are marked
'medium', 'hot' or 'very hot' to avoid
confusion among customers.

Papannis Wine Bistro

55 Strait Street (2125 1960). **Open**
Oct-June noon-2.30pm, 7-11pm Mon-Fri.
July-Sept noon-2.30pm Mon-Fri. **€€**.
Mediterranean. Map p50 C3 ㉝
A cosy trattoria set in a restored
Valletta townhouse and featuring an
open kitchen turning out the kind of
light lunch perfect for those seeking
extra energy for shopping or sightseeing. Start with a classic Maltese
antipasto – pickled Gozo cheese, broadbean dip, Maltese sausage, olives and
roasted tomatoes – before following it
up with a fresh salad, seafood pasta or
some seriously tasty risotto.

Phoenix Restaurant

*Le Méridien Phoenicia, The Mall,
Floriana (2291 1083).* **Open**
7-10.30am, 7-10.30pm daily. **€€€**.
Mediterranean. Map p50 A3 ㉞

MALTA BY AREA

Since chef Victor Borg returned to the Phoenix a few months ago, this chic hotel restaurant has been taken to even higher levels, with dining on a delightful terrace overlooking the Valletta bastions or within the smart 1930s-style interior. The menu is both innovative and refined: milk-fed veal is slow cooked to perfection and tender lamb is served with a black olive tapenade. The hotel also houses the Pegasus Brasserie for more informal dining in a casual, contemporary setting.

Da Pippo

136 Melita Street (2124 8029).
Open noon-4pm Mon-Sat. €€.
Mediterranean. Map p50 C3 ③⑤
An informal trattoria always packed with a loyal crowd and run by eminently friendly staff. Complimentary antipasti includes broad beans, olives and local cheese, while main courses include Maltese fare such as baked marrows stuffed with mincemeat alongside fresh fish and excellent pasta dishes. The downside is that tables are packed close together and it can get overwhelmingly crowded, not to mention noisy on weekends.

Rubino

53 Old Bakery Street (2122 4656).
Open 12.15-2.30pm Mon, Wed, Thur; 12.15-2.30pm, 7.45-10.30pm Tue, Fri. Closed Aug. €€. **Maltese. Map** p50 C3 ③⑥
Owned by Julian Sammut, cofounder of a company promoting Maltese cuisine, Rubino is among the island's finest when it comes to a fusion of traditional and modern Maltese cooking. Specialities include tuna cooked in a unique concoction of mint, vinegar and peppercorns, Maltese sausage stew, fried balls of herb-seasoned mince, baked lamb chops and broad bean soup with pasta. Be sure to end your meal with what may be the finest cassata siciliana on the islands.

Sicilia Bar & Restaurant

1 St John's Street (2124 0569).
Open 8am-6pm Tue-Sat. €€.
Italian. Map p50 C4 ③⑦

The food is far from life-changing, the service brisk and the Sicilians who run the place often end up throwing insults at each other, yet this remains a favourite haunt of Maltese families thanks to the delightful dining terrace with its views of the Grand Harbour. Seafood pasta is popular – try the house special with curried shrimps in cream, spinach and brandy – and there are plenty of Sicilian sweets with which to end the meal.

Spezzo

NEW *Civil Service Sports Club, 113 Archbishop Street (2122 8500).*
Open *Restaurant* 11.30am-2.30pm, 7-11pm daily. *Bar* 10am-1am daily. Closed Sun mid May-mid Sept. €€€.
Mediterranean. Map p51 D3 ③⑧
Old meets new at Spezzo, recently opened and boasting an atmosphere both elegant yet relaxed and a dining area that is large yet unusually intimate. The building's old Baroque edifice gives way to an arched space with thick columns, carvings and high ceilings, although the softly lit modern bar area adds a more contemporary touch. Suckling pig comes straight from the rotisserie, shellfish platters straight from the ocean outside, and there are some indulgent desserts.

Trabuxu

1 Strait Street (2122 3036). **Open** noon-2.30pm, 7pm-midnight Tue-Sat; 7pm-midnight Sun. **Bar. Map** p50 B3 ③⑨
Housed in a small vaulted cellar and offering an extensive and well-selected wine list, Trabuxu is most popular in winter, when the cosy interior truly comes into its own. Bar food includes platters of cheeses and cured meats, fondues, soups and various daily specials. Paintings by local and foreign artists are regularly exhibited on the thick stone walls and the staff are always happy to help recommend a wine by the glass or bottle.

2 22

NEW *222 Great Siege Road (2733 3222/www.two-twentytwo.com).* **Open** 12.30pm-1am daily. **Bar. Map** p50 B2 ④⓪

Lantern p61

The hippest place to hit the city this year. This historic building's barrel-vaulted interior has mercifully been kept intact and blends harmoniously with the minimalist design – the most striking feature of which is an illuminated cascade of water greeting you at the bar. Food is served downstairs, drinks and nibbles upstairs – try to grab a seat on the outdoor terrace to soak up the spectacular view of Valletta's bastions, steeples and domes. Bizarre video projections and increasingly upbeat electronic music lend a more clubby atmosphere as the party moves into the small hours.

Shopping

Agenda Bookshop

Valletta Waterfront (2122 7585).
Open *June-Sept* 9am-midnight daily.
Oct-May 9am-10pm Mon-Fri, Sun;
9am-midnight Sat. **Map** p50 A5 ④

The Agenda Bookshop chain has branches throughout Malta and carries what is undoubtedly the widest selection of books on the island. This outlet on the picturesque Valletta Waterfront is the largest, offering new titles, best-sellers and children's books, plus various background books on Malta and international magazines.

Artisans Centre

Freedom Square (2124 6216). **Open**
9am-7pm Mon-Fri; 9am-1pm Sat.
Map p50 B3 ④

Locally crafted silver items plus Gozo lace, original watercolours, brass door knockers and blown glass. Not all of the pieces for sale are actually made by Maltese artists, but feel free to ask and the staff will happily point out what's local and what's not.

Ascot House

243 Republic Street (2122 1372).
Open 9am-1pm, 4-7pm Mon-Fri;
9am-1pm Sat. **Map** p50 C3 ④

Men's designer labels in a smart corner shop facing one of Valletta's loveliest squares, with a large selection of formal shirts, ties, suits, underwear and accessories from the likes of Hugo Boss, Dolce & Gabbana, Versace and Cavalli. The less formal clothing collection is displayed at Ascot Casuals, right across the square.

Bubbles

257 Republic Street (2122 1935).
Open 9am-1.30pm, 4-7pm Mon-Fri;
9am-1.30pm Sat. **Map** p50 C3 ④

Don't get confused – the window of this delightful shoe shop is a few doors down from the outlet, which is up a

MALTA BY AREA

Time stands still

What makes traditional Maltese clockmakers tick?

Halfway down St Paul's Street in Valletta, a small doorway and eight stone steps lead to one of the city's best-kept secrets: a tiny workshop called **Gilder** (no.48, 9926 6433), where Dorian Dimech can be found tirelessly handcrafting majestic wall clocks in the same style that decorated the homes of Maltese nobles as far back as the 17th century.

The 38-year-old artisan was a soldier until a powerful calling eight years ago persuaded him to leave the armed forces and pursue his father's trade – something he'd rebelled against as a child – and now Mondays to Fridays find him opening the wooden shutters of his shop at 10am and indulging his hobby until 2pm.

And Dorian has clearly earned something of a reputation from satisfied customers along the way: word of mouth has spread beyond the islands and led to sales as far afield as Canada, South Korea, the UK and Russia. Not bad going when you stop and consider how easy it would be to blink and miss the door to his shop.

Not that you'd blink and miss the making of a Maltese clock. Each one is intricately crafted from wood before being engraved and gilded with varying amounts of 22-carat gold leaf on a dark background, and then decorated with floral motifs, seascapes or heraldic coats of arms.

Such items clearly make stylish Maltese gifts, but don't expect to pick one up for a song. In total, Dorian manufactures around ten clocks every year, which then sell for between €600 and €3,000 depending on the size of the clock, the intricacy of its design and the amount of gold leaf involved. Ask for a demonstration and Dorian might well remove the blue quilted cloth covering up his masterpiece – a red Maltese clock topped with a figure of St Paul and covered in intricate gold swirls (he used over eight books of gold leaf in the process) that will ultimately fetch well over €3,000.

'I put a lot of passion and accuracy into each timepiece,' says Dorian, and looking at his work it's easy to believe him.

steep flight of steps and sells what are probably the most beautiful shoes on the island. As the shop is small, the collection is extremely well edited: inexpensive casual shoes and a larger selection of smart, pricier shoes, many with matching bags.

C Camilleri & Sons Ltd

49-51 Merchants Street (2124 1642/ www.camillerigroup.com). **Open** 9am-1pm, 4-7pm Mon-Fri; 9am-1pm Sat; 9am-noon Sun. No credit cards. **Map** p50 C3/4 ⑤

Synonymous with sweetness for over 160 years, Camilleri offers the largest selection of sweets and chocolates on the island. For local delights, try the freshly baked almond cakes or seasonal specialities such as the Carnival *prinjolata* (creamy almond sponge cake coated with meringue and chocolate).

Chemimart

20 Republic Street (2124 6063). **Open** 9am-7pm Mon-Fri; 9am-8pm Sat. **Map** p50 B3 ⑥

A leading perfumery chain established for over 40 years and with branches throughout Malta, Chemimart stocks a range of designer fragrances from the likes of Calvin Klein, Armani, Ralph Lauren and Valentino, plus a good line in skin, hair and beauty products.

Classic Jewellers

293 Republic Street (2122 0200). **Open** 9am-7pm Mon-Sat; 9am-2pm Sun. **Map** p50 B3 ⑦

Plain jewellery in contemporary designs, intricate filigree, mounted stones, a selection of pearls and other pieces in silver, gold and white gold. This branch – one of a number throughout Malta – has its more expensive selection on the ground floor, with stunning classic and modern items from affordable to the ultra-expensive.

Cost Borg

250 Republic Street (2123 7363). **Open** 9am-6pm, 4-7pm Mon-Fri; 9am-1pm Sat. **Map** p50 C3 ⑧

Conservative gentlemen's clothing and accessories from the likes of Bridge,

Trussardi, Valentino, Burberry and Ermenegildo Zegna, all displayed in a wood-panelled shop with an aura of years gone by. Look out for the discounted items and don't miss the collection of informal shirts displayed in a small outlet across the road.

Darmanin

19 Republic Street (2124 4877). **Open** 9am-7.30pm Mon-Sat. **Map** p50 B3 ⑭

A successful shoe chain with branches across the island, Darmanin offers the largest selection of shoes for men, women and children at moderate prices. The outlet in Republic Street stocks exclusive one-off pairs of boots and shoes for the fashion-conscious (some with matching bags), as well as classic styles for traditionalists.

Diamonds International

293 Republic Street (2122 0200/www. diamondsinternational.com.mt). **Open** 9am-7pm Mon-Sat. **Map** p50 B3 ⑤

Diamonds take pride of place in this elegant marble-floored outlet where gorgeous designer pieces are showcased in stylish displays, but there are also stunning pearl creations, watches, cufflinks and accessories from highly respectable brands such as Cartier, Christian Dior and Mont Blanc.

Diesel Store

222 Merchants Street (2123 7782). **Open** *June-Aug* 10am-7.30pm Mon-Sat. *Sept-May* 9.30am-2pm, 4-7pm Mon-Sat. **Map** p50 C3 ⑤

Two stores on opposite sides of the road between them offer T-shirts, jeans and jackets for the young and audacious, plus a range of stylish skirts for the girls. The famous Italian label's effortlessly casual look is enhanced by a collection of funky accessories including belts, watches, shoes, sunglasses and underwear, and the place is popular with Malta's poseable teens.

Early Learning Centre

193 Merchants Street (2123 6228/ www.elc.co.uk). **Open** 9am-12.30pm, 4-7pm Mon-Fri; 9am-12.30pm Sat. **Map** p50 C3 ⑤

MALTA BY AREA

A shop promoting learning through play in children up to six years old. Rest assured that every item – from traditional wooden toys to electronic instruments – has an educational purpose, with each one individually marked with a unique 'Early Learning Icon' to indicate the key skills it aims to develop in children.

Edwards Lowell Co Ltd
6-7 Zachary Street (2124 4159).
Open 9.30am-1pm, 4.30-7pm Mon-Fri; 9.30am-1pm Sat. **Map** p50 B3 ⑥③
You have to ring a bell to gain access to this chicest of shops, a small family-run business stocking only the finest watches and jewellery for both men and women, and from major names along the lines of Rolex, Raymond Weil, Breitling and Patek Philippe.

Embassy Complex
Santa Lucia Street (2122 7436).
Open 9am-1pm, 4-7pm Mon-Sat.
Map p50 C3 ⑥④
In the heart of Valletta's retail district stands the capital's main shopping complex, home to quality outlets like Accessorise, Monsoon, United Colors of Benetton, Agenda Bookshop, Pedigree Toyshop and new addition Missha, the make-up specialist. The complex also houses a bar, cinema and major tourist attraction the Wartime Experience (p57), all located on the upper floors of the building.

Franco Bajada
192 Merchants Street (2123 7948).
Open 8.30am-1pm, 4-7pm Mon-Fri; 8.30am-1pm Sat. **Map** p50 C3 ⑥⑤
This small, well-stocked outlet oozes Italian style with clothes to dress up the elegant, mature man for any occasion – tailored suits, shirts, ties, scarves, cufflinks and hats. Ask the kindly owner for assistance as not all items are easily visible.

Gio Batta Delia
Ferreria Palace, 307 Republic Street (2123 3618). **Open** 9.30am-1.30pm, 4-6.30pm Mon-Fri; 9.30am-12.30pm Sat. **Map** p50 B3 ⑥⑥

Housed within the beautiful Palazzo Ferreria, Gio Batta Delia is the most well established crystal and china store across Malta, displaying a beautiful selection of designer pieces by Wedgwood alongside other major international names such as Baccarat, Waterford, Royal Copenhagen, Royal Worcester and Spode.

Kenjo & Kyoto
128 & 52 Old Theatre Street (2122 0724/2125 0264). **Open** 9am-1pm, 4-7pm Mon-Sat. **Map** p51 D3 ⑥⑦
Women who want to stun with their outfits tend to shop at Kenjo or Kyoto, located opposite each other and between them selling everything from tailored morning suits to stylish evening dresses. Both outlets are rather small but stocked with a fantastic selection of elegant womenswear from labels such as Ella Donna, Lexus, Bain de Nuit and Max Azria.

Mango
Britannia Centre, Santa Lucia Street (2122 2951). **Open** 9.30am-7pm Mon-Thur; 9am-7pm Fri, Sat. **Map** p50 C3 ⑥⑧
This popular Spanish womenswear chain is laid out over three floors, starting off with casual clothing and moving up to more stylish garments, with classic suits and glamorous eveningwear on the upper floors. From plain T-shirts to glitzy dresses, the eclectic range appeals to women of all ages, styles and tastes. There is also a collection of shoes, bags and other accessories to complete the look.

Marks & Spencer
Palace Square (2123 1217). **Open** 9am-7pm Mon-Sat. **Map** p50 C3 ⑥⑨
This popular branch of the British high street staple M&S is an obvious destination for quality basics such as underwear, nightwear and T-shirts, but has in recent years extended its appeal to the young and fashion-conscious by spicing up its collection with contemporary designs for both men and women. There is a café and small food store on the ground floor for refreshment between fittings.

MALTA BY AREA

Mdina Glass

*Valletta Waterfront (2141 5786/
www.mdinaglass.net).* **Open** 10am-
10pm daily. **Map** p50 A5 ⑥⓪

A long-standing seller of all things
hand-crafted – from candles and coast-
ers to vases, clocks and mirrors –
Mdina Glass has in recent years
expanded its line to include contemporary and colourful designs. Prices are
hefty, especially for the more modern
pieces, but the pedigree of the items on
offer is never in question.

Mexx

Republic Street (2202 2152). **Open**
9am-7pm Mon-Sat. **Map** p50 C3 ⑥①

Linen is once again in at Mexx, with an
informal and casually flattering collection largely informed by soft, neutral
colours. The outlet stretches over three
floors and features a range of accessories from jewellery, belts and bags to
pretty, strappy shoes.

Miss Sixty

50 Santa Lucia Street (2122 4809).
Open 9.30am-1.30pm, 4-7pm Mon-Sat.
Map p50 C3 ⑥②

A bright range of figure-hugging
clothes for hip young girls looking for
feminine wear with a funky twist that
they know will get noticed. The label's
famous fitted jeans are on the ground
floor of this small outlet, and in summer there's also a good selection of
swimwear on display.

Morgan

218 Merchants Street (2122 7905).
Open 9am-7pm Mon-Fri; 9am-2pm Sat.
Map p50 C3 ⑥③

Flirty tops, hip-hugging skirts and
sleek dresses: this world-beating
French label offers an ultra-feminine
and provocative collection for all sea-
sons, and allows wearers to comple-
ment their look with an equally
attractive range of accessories.

OK Gifts

Kingsway Palace, Republic Street (2123 6356/www.oklimited.com). **Open** 9am-7pm Mon-Fri; 9am-1pm Sat. **Map** p50 C3 ⑥④

Graceful Lladró statuettes, a fascinating range of delicate crystal items by Swarovski and a selection of locally blown glass are among the pieces on display at this delightful corner shop. Look out for the new collection of contemporary fashion jewellery sculpted largely with silver and diamonds.

Pedigree Toyshops

Valletta Waterfront (2122 6800). **Open** 9am-9pm daily. **Map** p50 A5 ⑥⑤

Set on two floors in a high-vaulted building initially constructed by the Knights, this branch of the island-wide Pedigree Toyshop chain combines a wide array of toys and games for children of all ages with a selection of local souvenirs including blown glass, ceramic items and lacework.

Piccinino

239 Republic Street (2123 6753). **Open** 9am-1pm, 4-7pm Mon-Sat. **Map** p50 C3 ⑥⑥

An underwear outlet specialising in sexy lingerie and swimwear for more discerning customers. Women of all shapes and contours are catered for, from AA up to H cups, with bikini tops and bottoms available separately for the proportionally challenged. That said, larger women are better off in the branch on Merchants Street, where sizes go up to J cup.

Sandro Azzopardi Gioielleria

45 Zachary Street (2122 7185/www. sandroazzopardi.com). **Open** 9.30am-1pm, 4-6.45pm Mon-Fri; 9.30am-1pm Sat. **Map** p50 B3 ⑥⑦

A classy marble-fronted jewellery store in Valletta's prettiest shopping street, with a wide range of exclusive items for people with good taste and deep pockets – Bulgari, Chaumet and Vacheron Constantin are among the designers represented, with some items by Sandro Azzopardi himself.

Sapienza's Bookshop

26 Republic Street (2123 3621). **Open** 9am-7pm Mon-Fri; 9am-1pm Sat. **Map** p50 C3 ⑥⑧

This small, eminently friendly bookstore covers two levels and has an extensive collection of books about the history and culture of Malta, as well as a wide variety of English-language titles covering everything from classics and children's books to commercial fiction and non-fiction.

Segue

29 Old Treasury Street (2122 7788). **Open** *May-Sept* 9am-7pm Mon-Fri; 9am-1pm Sat. *Oct-Apr* 9am-1.30pm, 4-7pm Mon-Fri; 9am-1pm Sat. **Map** p50 C3 ⑥⑨

It's not the easiest shop to find (tucked rather disarmingly down a narrow alley near the National Library), but Segue displays a wide selection of well-priced, high-quality bags from names like Sisley and United Colors of Benetton – prices start from around €23. A small selection of wallets, gloves, scarves and other accessories is also available.

La Senza

Level 3, Energy Complex, Republic Street (2123 8491). **Open** 9am-7pm Mon-Sat. **Map** p50 C3 ⑦⓪

This high street lingerie label has only recently hit Malta, but locals are already swearing by its range of inexpensive lingerie and nightwear, which covers all corners of the spectrum from the comfortably functional to the downright saucy.

Solaris

281 Republic Street (2123 2955/ www.solaris.fr). **Open** 9.30am-7pm Mon-Sat. **Map** p50 C3 ⑦①

A sunglasses specialist stocking designer brands including Gucci, Versace, Cartier, Prada and Dior. Feel free to try on any model – the store offers unassisted access to everything on display – and rest assured that Solaris also guarantees the effectiveness of all its sunglasses in the fight against harmful UV rays.

MALTA BY AREA

Sterling Jewellers

6D Republic Street (2124 4085).
Open 9am-7pm Mon-Fri; 9am-1pm
Sat. **Map** p50 B3 72

With branches across the island,
Sterling Jewellers offers items for all
budgets in both classic and modern
designs. The traditional Maltese cross
remains the most popular buy – available in silver or gold, either plain or
encrusted with stones – but there are
plenty more contemporary items by
international designers.

Victor Azzopardi Jewellers

*31, 32, 34 St Anne Street, Floriana
(2123 3715/www.victorazzopardi.com).*
Open 9.30am-1pm, 4-7pm Mon-Fri;
9.30am-1pm Sat. **Map** p50 A3 73

Victor Azzopardi and family have been
selling unique items for well over a century. This outlet displays a wonderful
collection of Maltese silverwear including teapots, oil lamps and candelabras,
plus a range of fine jewellery by top
international designers such as Paul
Picot, Lancaster and Kenzo.

Arts & leisure

Embassy Cinema

*Santa Lucia Street (2122 2225/
www.embassycomplex.com.mt).* **Open**
according to screenings. **Map** p50 C3 74

Set on the top floors of Valletta's main
shopping complex, the Embassy
Cinema shows mainstream Hollywood
releases throughout the day and long
into the evening, with cutting-edge
sound and projection facilities and a
clean, friendly environment.

Manoel Theatre

*Old Theatre Street (2124 6389/www.
teatrumanoel.com.mt).* **Open** *Tours*
10.30am, 11.30am, 1.15pm Mon-Fri;
11.30am, 12.30pm Sat. *Performances*
times vary. **Map** p51 D3 75

One of Europe's oldest surviving theatres, construction of the Manoel was
personally funded by the wealthy
Grand Master Manoel de Vilhena in
1731. It is designed in an elegant oval
shape, with 600 seats and row upon
row of intimate boxes finished with

flamboyant Baroque carvings, and
with acoustics so fine that even those
in the auditorium can hear conductors
turning the pages of their score. There
is also a souvenir shop and a lovely
courtyard café serving fresh snacks
and divine Italian gelati. The programme is mostly dedicated to classical music: check the website or booking
office for details of forthcoming plays,
concerts and other performances.

Mediterranean Conference Centre

Valletta (2559 5215/www.mcc.com.mt).
Open times vary. **Map** p51 E4 76

Located on the periphery of the capital
and overlooking the Grand Harbour,
the Mediterranean Conference Centre
is a 16th-century building formerly
known as the 'Sacra Infermeria' of the
Order of St John. In its modern incarnation it caters for up to 1,400 delegates
across ten halls and nine syndicate
rooms, hosting everything from conferences and product launches to exhibitions and conventions. The centre also
often stages cultural events such as
dance and music festivals, operas, concerts and plays – check the website for
details of forthcoming events.

St James Cavalier Centre for Creativity

*Pope Pius V Street (2122 3200/
www.sjcav.org).* **Open** 10am-9pm
daily. No credit cards. **Map** p50 B4 77

Malta's contemporary arts centre is set
in a defensive fortress built by the
Knights to counteract land attacks.
The 11 former ammunition chambers
are today a perfect setting for exhibition halls that host temporary modern
art exhibitions from painting and
installation to photography, ceramics
and glasswork by mostly Maltese
artists. For an updated list of current
and upcoming exhibitions check the
website. The affiliated 60-seat St James
Cavalier Theatre stages a range of
mostly English-language plays, while
the single-screen St James Cavalier
Cinema is the only venue in Malta dedicated to foreign and arthouse films.

MALTA BY AREA

Balluta Bay

St Julian's & Paceville

Initially a small fishing village, St Julian's today spreads along the picturesque coast encompassing the bays of Balluta, Spinola and St George's. It holds the single largest concentration of restaurants and hotels in Malta, while central Paceville is the beating heart of the island's nightlife scene, teeming with clubs, bars and casinos and often noisy until the small hours.

A large square at Balluta Bay marks the point where St Julian's merges imperceptibly with Sliema, and is also home to two notable buildings: the neo-Gothic Carmelite Church with its long spindly bell towers, and Balluta Buildings, a florid and weathered but still monumental apartment block that marks the legacy of Malta's brief flirtation with art nouveau, its sculpted façade embellished with repeated angel motifs and elegant flying buttresses.

Bustling Spinola Bay takes its name from a nearby Baroque palace built by Giovanni Battista Spinola, a bailiff of the Order of St John. A number of old boathouses skirting along one side of the bay continue to serve the small community of local fishermen, although many shore buildings and boathouses have been converted into restaurants. Spinola's beauty is most striking in the evening, with the street lights reflected in a bay rippling with the weight of so many traditional wooden boats.

Various upmarket hotels line the coast north of Spinola Bay, among them Malta's highest building, the Portomaso tower, looming over a yacht marina set in an artificial inlet. Further inland, more party-hearty punters will only too happily stumble upon Paceville, a criss-cross of streets packed with bars, clubs, casinos, cinemas and informal eateries where the majority of Malta's young and up-for-it congregate of an evening. The place gets crowded every night, overwhelmingly so in the summer months, with parties regularly carrying on in the streets after the clubs kick out at 4am – somewhere to avoid, then, for those seeking a romantic or family break.

North of Paceville is St George's Bay, a small, sandy beach popular with foreign fun-lovers during both the day and at night, dominated by a thick fringe of upmarket hotels and **Paranga**, a stylish bar and restaurant that many see as the perfect starting point for a long night on the tiles.

Eating & drinking

Alley

Wilga Street, Paceville (7992 2199). **Open** 8pm-4am daily. **Bar**. Map p72 B2 ❶

A perennially heaving rock bar that has retained a unique underground identity despite several refurbishments. Rock aficionados flock to the acoustic sessions every Wednesday and the live gigs on Fridays, plus the Alley is the only bar in Malta with an in-house recording studio, giving local bands an opportunity to lay down tracks of their own.

Al Molo

NEW *Portomaso, St Julian's (2138 4300).* **Open** 7-11pm Mon-Sat. **€€€**. **Italian**. Map p72 B2 ❷

This recent addition to the local eating scene offers healthy yet flavoursome Italian dishes made with seasonal ingredients, although vegetarians will need to ask the chef to prepare something especially (meat and fish dishes prevail). Alongside friendly staff, quick service and a refreshingly modern interior, Al Molo also enjoys one of Malta's best locations beside Portomaso marina and has a large alfresco terrace.

Amigos

Wilga Street, Paceville (2137 6807). **Open** noon-2am Mon-Thur, Sun; noon-6am Fri, Sat. **€**. **Mexican**. Map p72 B2 ❸

First opened in Sliema as a Mexican fast-food joint, Amigos did so well that it set up this second outlet in the heart of Paceville to cater for hungry nightgoers on the prowl for after-pub sustenance. Pizzas, fajitas and tacos are cooked to perfection and the ingredients are incredibly fresh, plus there's seating for those who'd rather eat in. **Other location** Dingli Street, Dingli Circus, Sliema (2133 2480).

Avenue

Paceville Avenue, Paceville (2135 1753/www.theavenuemalta.com). **Open** noon-2.30pm, 6-11.30pm Mon-Sat; 6-11.30pm Sun. **€€**. **Italian**. Map p72 B2/3 ❹

This enormous Italian eaterie has been serving quality, affordable food for time out of mind, including spaghetti with sea urchins (when in season), pasta della casa with chunks of fillet beef and farfalle 'Popeye' with spinach, bacon and mushrooms. Peak times see queues for tables, so book ahead.

Bar Native

St Rita Steps, St George's Road, Paceville (2138 0635). **Open** 7pm-4am daily. **Bar**. Map p72 A2 ❺

This Native American-themed bar has waiter service and a great cocktail menu, plus music that quickly switches from chilled to floor-filling once local DJs have taken over from the jukebox. The lounge bar area inside offers a laid-back atmosphere and a smoking section, while summer sees drinkers spilling out on to the terraced seating and mingling with passers-by.

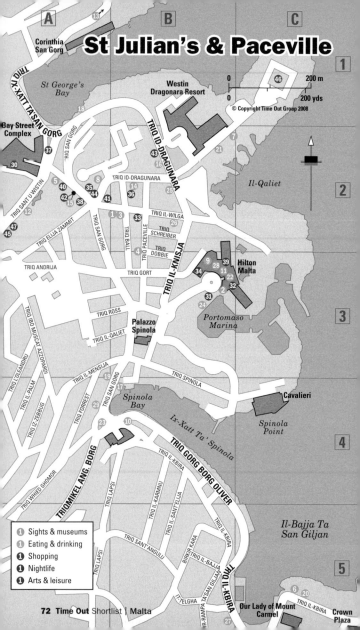

St Julian's & Paceville

Corinthia
San Gorg

St George's
Bay

Westin
Dragonara Resort

Bay Street
Complex

Il-Qaliet

TRIQ ID-DRAGUNARA

TRIQ SAN GORG

TRIQ SANT U WISTIN

TRIQ ID-DRAGUNARA

TRIQ IL-WILGA

TRIQ SCHREIBER

TRIQ ELIJA ZAMMIT

TRIQ SAN GORG

TRIQ BALL

TRIQ PACEVILLE

TRIQ DOBBIE

TRIQ IL-KNISJA

Hilton
Malta

TRIQ ANDRIJA

TRIQ GORT

Portomaso
Marina

TRIQ ROSS

Palazzo
Spinola

TRIQ IL-QALIET

TRIQ IBO MUSCAT AZZOPARDI

TRIQ IL-MENSIJA

TRIQ SAN GORG

TRIQ SPINOLA

Cavalieri

TRIQ LOLEANDRU

TRIQ IL-PALM

TRIQ IZ-ZEBBUG

TRIQ FORREST

Spinola
Bay

Ix-Xatt Ta' Spinola

Spinola
Point

TRIQMIKEL ANG. BORG

TRIQ WHIED GHOMOR

TRIQ GORG BORG OLIVER

TRIQ IL-KBIRA

TRIQ LAPSI

TRIQ IL-KARMNU

TRIQ IL-SANT'ELIJA

TRIQ IL-KBIRA

Il-Bajja Ta
San Giljan

TRIQ SANT'ANGLU

BIRKIRKARA

TRIQ IL-BAJJA

IR-RAMPA TA SAN GILJAN

IT-TELGHA

TRIQ IL-KBIRA

Our Lady of Mount
Carmel

Crown
Plaza

1 Sights & museums
1 Eating & drinking
1 Shopping
1 Nightlife
1 Arts & leisure

0   200 m
0   200 yds

© Copyright Time Out Group 2008

Barracuda

194-195 Main Street, St Julian's (2133 1817/www.wgc-group.com). **Open** *May-Sept* 7-11pm daily. *Oct-Apr* 7-11pm Mon-Sat. **€€€. Mediterranean.** Map p72 C5 ⑥

One of the most elegant restaurants this side of the island, Barracuda offers a stylish white interior on the water's edge with a lovely terrace for alfresco dining. Fish is a notable highlight, from an intensely flavoured lobster bisque starter to the display cabinet from which you can pick your own catch of the day for the main. Madonna, Sharon Stone and David Beckham are among those Barracuda has snapped up in the past.

Bedouin Bar

Westin Dragonara Resort, St Julian's (2138 1000). **Open** *June-Sept* 7pm-1am daily. **Bar.** Map p72 B2 ⑦

Open in summer only, Bedouin Bar offers visitors the chance to party right on the water's edge, its Moroccan theme bolstered with furnishings flown direct from Marrakech, from floor cushions to shisha pipes. A beach club by day, by night the bar becomes a laid-back lounge spot and – towards the end of the week – a happening party venue, with resident DJs dropping house anthems every Friday to a normally packed dancefloor.

Blackbull

Dragonara Road, Paceville (2137 1363). **Open** noon-4am daily. **Pub.** Map p72 A2 ⑧

This Irish pub and grill is a great place to sit and people-watch thanks to its pavement seating on one of Malta's busiest thoroughfares. Sporting events are screened daily, with a largely expat crowd lounging around drinking and dining at leisure, although once the sun goes down the party is on and there's dancing both inside and on the street.

Blue Elephant

Hilton Malta, Portomaso, St Julian's (2138 3383/www.blueelephant.com/malta). **Open** 7-11pm daily. **€€€. Thai.** Map p72 B2 ⑨

From the wooden bridges and waterfalls to the exotic plants, burnished brass crockery and courteous, mostly Thai staff, dining at the Blue Elephant is an exercise in spoiling yourself, and there's no better way to do it in style than with the four-course Ruby of Siam or Royal Thai Banquet set menus – feasts for eyes and taste buds alike. Both incorporate the restaurant's best dishes, from green prawn and chicken curries to scallops in oyster sauce.

Dubliner Irish Pub & Restaurant

Spinola Bay, St Julian's (2136 7106). **Open** 11am-2am Mon-Thur; 11am-4am Fri-Sun. **Pub.** Map p72 B4 ⑩

An Englishman and an Irishman walk into a bar… or rather, they open one. The owners of the Dubliner have a soft spot for their regulars, but tourists will find the place just as accommodating, regardless of whether they opt for a bite to eat in the upstairs restaurant or a more casual night in the ground-floor bar. Big screen sports garner much effusive cheering from the hordes of Guinness-fuelled locals.

Dusk Lounge Bar

NEW *Portomaso, St Julian's (2138 9289).* **Open** 8am-2am daily. **Bar.** Map p72 B2 ⑪

A large, welcoming bar with ample leather armchairs and a small terrace with stunning views over Portomaso's marina. A detailed wine list helpfully describes over 300 bottles in stock, and there's also a decent cocktail menu. Quiet throughout winter, Dusk picks up in the summer months with a mix of clients of all ages, both local and less so. Snacks come in the form of platters from neighbouring Portomaso restaurants and include local cheeses, fish and cold cuts, plus there's also great sushi.

Eastern Breeze

InterContinental Hotel, St George's Bay, St Julian's (2137 7600). **Open** 7-11pm daily. **€€€. Asian.** Map p72 A2 ⑫

A restaurant with an elegant wooden interior and a menu that's big on quality Asian platters like the Seven Sins

MALTA BY AREA

Our people are key to finding your dream holiday home.

Tony Scicluna +356 9942 8587 Elayne Cuschieri +356 9925 0999 Darren Frendo +356 7959 5243 Manuel Pace +356 9985 6761 Veronica Sapiano +356 9931 6907 David Schembri +356 9946 4816 Roberta Schembri +356 9949 7100 Clive Demicoll +356 9949 7735 John Vella +356 7949 4443 Joe Woods +356 7949 7508 Tracy Mann +356 9927 9145 Erskine Vella +356 9944 9606 Anthony Baldwin +356 9945 3808 Adrian Ellul +356 9955 5508 Jerry Ellul +356 7942 9165 Darren Micallef +356 9947 5037 Omar Xuereb +356 9947 8279 Josianne Zerafa +356 9929 5955 Laura Paun +356 9945 6121 Franco Tabone +356 7970 2161 Benji Psaila +356 9920 2030 Janice Balzan +356 9944 4858 Matthew Barry +356 7945 1411 Matthew Buff +356 9929 6924 Francesca Tabone +356 9944 7704 Gerald Gouder +356 7949 4923 Gordon Attard +356 7943 1977 Angelo Borg +356 7942 1340 Edward Cachia +356 7989 5131 Fabien Debono +356 7925 2236 Max Magri +356 9947 5444 Patrick Pace +356 7942 3568 John Zammit +356 7989 3252 Warren Azzopardi +356 7947 0327 Sandra Grech +356 7947 8108 Damian Whitehead +356 7942 0274 Desmond Scerri +356 9983 1607 Reuben Chircop St John +356 9906 0206 Darren Abela +356 7947 7497 Jeffrey Solberra +356 7989 2914 Damian Galea +356 7945 7082 Sean James Abela +356 7927 9855 Dennis Cilia +356 9940 9320 Anton Gauci +356 9940 4334 Joseph Sammut +356 7905 5248 Laura Sammut +356 9942 7372 Michael Mifsud +356 9947 0881 Alex Ellul +356 9947 2000 Anthony Gera +356 7982 0533 Martin Mercieca +356 7942 9711 Carlo Paesano +356 9947 5434 Steve Schembri +356 9940 1515 Neville Sciberras +356 9949 4851 Joseph Agius +356 7947 1661 Mark Borg Manglon +356 9983 0000 Philip Incorvaja 7942 6774 Kajal Narwani +356 7937 3187 Mauro Sammut +356 9931 9100 Fredrick Stivala +356 9949 1074 Robert Farrugia +356 7983 8635 Konrad Sultana +356 9903 0767 Gordon Dalli +356 7921 9696 Kelvin John Goodwin +356 9945 6442 Christopher Zarb +356 9930 4288 Aldo Briffa +356 7965 9777 Nicky Camilleri +356 9942 9161 Steve Falzon +356 7325 1874 Ivan Cardona +356 9942 5798 Jean Pierre Attard +356 7982 4338

dhalia
real estate services

At Dhalia we genuinely try to make your world a better place to live in. With 11 offices around Malta and Gozo and 70 professional consultants, you will always be our most important customer and friend. Dhalia, Malta's real estate agency of choice.

+356 2149 0681 | info@dhalia.com | www.dhalia.com

Birkirkara | Fgura | Marsascala | St Julians | St Pauls Bay | Sliema
The Strand | Vittoriosa | Victoria - Gozo | Luxury Living by Dhalia

Fusion, a varied assortment of bite-sized prawn, chicken and duck parcels with accompanying sauces. Asian fish dishes are also lovingly prepared, with ridiculously fresh sushi and sashimi coming as standard.

Henry J Beans

Corinthia San Gorg, St George's Bay, St Julian's (2137 8239). **Open** 6pm-midnight Mon-Fri; noon-1am Sat, Sun. **€€**. **American**. Map p72 A1 ⑬

Henry J Beans is loud and proud, with young bartenders juggling bottles, a bell ringing every time a dish comes flying out the kitchen and – on weekends – a DJ keeping the dancefloor moving from his central stand. It's a great place to watch football with a burger and a beer, while in summer the bayside terrace is a lovely spot to sip a more cultured cocktail.

Huggins

Dragonara Road, Paceville (2137 5443/ www.hugginspub.com). **Open** 9am-midnight daily. **Bar**. Map p72 B2 ⑭

Popular day and night, especially with tourists, Huggins is the only place in the nightlife district serving breakfast, lunch and dinner, and also does a decent impression of a club when the DJ takes to the turntables later in the evening. Regular drinks promotions help things spiral out of control in the best possible way.

Hugo's Lounge

St George's Road, Paceville (2138 2264/www.hugosloungemalta.com). **Open** noon-1am Mon-Thur; noon-3am Fri-Sun. **€€**. **Asian**. Map p72 A2 ⑮

Strategically located and serving food until late in a chic and cheerful atmosphere, Hugo's is a stylish sushi and noodle restaurant with all the buzz of a bar. The recent addition of Malta's first sushi train (evenings only) allows for fine dining without the fuss, while more formal seated meals offer mains such as fresh tuna with ginger and desserts like the sublime ginger, chocolate and coconut ice cream. The uppermost floor of the building is home to the new club Shadow Lounge (p82).

Palm Beach

Dragonara Road, Paceville (2137 5331). **Open** noon-4am daily. **Bar**. Map p72 B2 ⑯

A spacious open-air bar popular with young crowds and foreign students, Palm Beach comes into its own in summer thanks to its patented wooden gazebos (which can and should be pre-booked), with white curtains, cosy mattresses, cushions and low lighting making for a luxurious, laid-back atmosphere. Pizzas constitute the majority of bar snacks and the music leans towards dance and uptempo pop.

Paparazzi

159 St George's Street, St Julian's (2137 4965). **Open** 9am-midnight daily. **€€**. **Mediterranean**. Map p72 B4 ⑰

On sunny days, locals and tourists alike flock to Paparazzi's outdoor terrace with its spectacular views of St George's Bay; when the weather is less clement, its American-themed interior – with gilded mirrors, wood panelling and Marilyn Monroe posters – is just as welcoming. Meat and fish dishes are available alongside a huge variety of pastas and pizzas, including a Maltese version with native sausage and gooey *gbejna* cheese – local comfort food at its most comforting.

Paranga

InterContinental Hotel, St George's Bay, St Julian's (2137 7600). **Open** May-Sept 7.30-11pm daily. **€€**. **Mediterranean**. Map p72 A1 ⑱

Set on a waterside teak deck overlooking St George's Bay, Paranga is elegant yet relaxed, with an upmarket yacht-like ambience and an abundance of light Mediterranean dishes suitable for summer evenings. There's also an excellent seafood menu, including flavoursome fish soup starters and grilled fish or shellfish platter mains.

Peppino's Restaurant & Wine Bar

31 St George's Street, St Julian's (2137 3200). **Open** noon-2.30pm, 7-11pm Mon-Sat. **€€**. **Mediterranean**. Map p72 A3/4 ⑲

MALTA BY AREA

Hugo's Lounge p75

Peppino's has a unique character thanks to its exquisite food, homely atmosphere and friendly, hands-on owners, who know their loyal clients by name and remember their individual preferences. Food is served either in the bar area or in the more formal first- and second-floor restaurants. When in doubt, plump for daily specials such as pasta with prawns and pistachios or grilled calamari served with rocket and fresh fish.

Piccolo Padre

195 Main Street, St Julian's (2134 4875/ www.wgc-group.com). **Open** 6.30-11pm daily. *Oct-Apr* 6.30-11pm Mon-Fri; 12.30-3.30pm, 6.30-11pm Sat, Sun. **€€**. **Italian**. Map p72 C5 ⑳

A cheerful pizza and pasta spot that's located beneath Barracuda restaurant (p73), Piccolo Padre is best known for the *pizzotto* – a rolled pizza with sesame seeds, blue cheese, onions, mushrooms, mozzarella and honey – but has also recently introduced a special line of healthy pizzas. In summer there's plenty of peaceful outdoor seating with tranquil sea views, plus a covered terrace for less clement alfresco eating experiences.

Quadro

Westin Dragonara Resort, Dragonara Road, St Julian's (2138 1000). **Open** noon-2.30pm, 7.30-11pm Mon-Fri; 7.30-11pm Sat, Sun. **€€€**. **Mediterranean**. Map p72 B2 ㉑

An outstanding restaurant with splendid views to heighten the dining experience. Quadro, set in the grounds of the imposing Westin Dragonara Resort, is one of Malta's most elegant eateries, home to veteran gourmet chef Michael Cauchi, whose trademark fish platter has been wooing loyal customers for years. Other culinary creations include grilled monkfish with pink grapefruit and duck leg confit with sesame and fig purée, and each month Michael puts together a four-course meal with a different glass of wine to accompany each course.

Quarterdeck Bar

Hilton Malta, Portomaso, St Julian's (2138 3383). **Open** 7pm-1.30am daily. **Bar**. Map p72 B3 ㉒

A classy bar located within the five-star Hilton Malta, sandwiched comfortably between the buzzing nightlife district of Paceville and the more picturesque stretches of Spinola Bay. The

MALTA BY AREA

Quarterdeck is ideal for a romantic sundowner and enjoys stunning views of the man-made marina below, stacked with luxury yachts, as well as the smart apartments of Portomaso.

Ryan's Irish Bar

Spinola Bay, St Julian's (2135 0680/ www.ryans.com.mt). **Open** 4pm-3am daily. **Pub**. Map p72 A4 ㉓

Big screen football and rugby events across the calendar see sports aficionados flock to Ryan's Irish Bar, perched on the hill above Spinola Bay, with cheering and chanting fuelled by lovingly poured pints of the black stuff. Live bands bring the noise on weekends and there's a charming outdoor terrace for those customers in search of a more tranquil tipple.

Sale e Pepe

Portomaso, St Julian's (2137 2918). **Open** *July-Sept* 7-11pm daily. *Oct-June* 7-11pm Mon-Sat; noon-3pm Sun. **€€**. **Mediterranean**. Map p72 B3 ㉔

Trattoria-like Sale e Pepe puts the Mediterranean good life on a plate, with pizza, pasta and flavoursome fish dishes served either indoors or on the alfresco terrace with sweeping marina views. The Maltese antipasti is exquisite – dips, olives, marinated artichokes, seafood and Gozo cheese.

Shiva's

[NEW] *8 Dragonara Road, Paceville (2138 4399).* **Open** 6.30-11pm Mon, Tue-Sun. **€€**. **Indian**. Map p72 B2 ㉕

A recent addition to Malta's roster of Indian restaurants, Shiva's is also undoubtedly among its finest. The naan breads are light and fluffy, and many of the sizzling mains come straight from the tandoori oven, including chicken, lamb, beef and seafood. Food is firmly pitched at the milder end of the spectrum, so if you like it spicy, ask for added kick.

Tana del Lupo

58A Wilga Street, Paceville (2135 3294). **Open** 7.15-11pm Mon; 12.15-2.30pm, 7.15-11pm Tue-Sat; 12.15-2.30pm Sun. **€€**. **Italian**. Map p72 B2 ㉖

Tana del Lupo is a traditional Sicilian restaurant frequented by local Italians who lap up the mixed seafood platters, fantastic pasta dishes and grilled fish mains while loudly setting the world to rights in their native tongue. Portions are smaller and prices slightly higher than elsewhere, but it's hard to beat for Italian authenticity.

Villa Brasserie

39 Main Street, Balluta Bay (2311 2233). **Open** noon-2.30pm, 7-11pm daily. **€€€**. **Mediterranean**. Map p72 B5 ㉗

The sweeping staircase, spacious terrace and grandiose balconies of this looming villa provide a striking contrast to the forward-thinking interior, where the walls are adorned with modern murals replicated in the matching crockery, and you'll even find a separate menu for bottled drinking water. Service is excellent and the brasserie food big on refined Mediterranean flavours: lamb shanks, cooked for hours, trios of seasonal fish and a range of sublime desserts.

Zeri's

Portomaso, St Julian's (2135 9559). **Open** 7-11pm Tue-Sun. **€€€**. **Fusion**. Map p72 B3 ㉘

Recently relocated to a spot it truly deserves – a simple, spacious restaurant with natural tones in the elegant Portomaso complex – Zeri's continues to cook up delicious Mediterranean dishes with an oriental twist. Fish is a speciality, from a crisp calamari salad to an outstanding involtini with salmon and sea bass.

Zest

Hotel Juliani, 12 St George's Road, Spinola Bay, St Julian's (2138 8000/ www.zestflavours.com). **Open** *June-Sept* 7-11.30pm daily. *Oct-May* 7-11.30pm Mon-Sat. **€€€**. **Fusion**. Map p72 A4 ㉙

Cutting-edge contemporary design, East-West fusion dishes and a hip, high-heeled crowd make an evening at Zest a real treat. Sushi fans can sit at the central bar and watch the Japanese chefs at work, while more formal seated

The best guides to enjoying London life

(but don't just take our word for it)

'Armed with a tube map and this guide there is no excuse to find yourself in a duff bar again'

Evening Standard

'I'm always asked how I keep up to date with shopping and services in a city as big as London. This guide is the answer'

Red Magazine

'You will never again be stuck for interesting things to do and places to visit in the capital'

Independent on Sunday

Rated 'Best Restaurant Guide'

Sunday Times

TIME OUT GUIDES WRITTEN BY LOCAL EXPERTS
timeout.com/shop

Age of ascent

Learning the ropes with Malta's monsters of rock.

It may be better known as a destination for divers, but a new generation of tourists is choosing to scale Malta's rocky heights rather than plumb its watery depths, with countless faces of all shapes and sizes offering some of the best and most accessible climbing in Europe.

'Most climbing destinations have one overcrowded "super crag" that every climber flocks to,' says Ian Frith, president of the London Mountaineering Club, which organises regular trips to the islands. 'Malta is unique for the sheer range of climbing spots on offer over all three islands – it's never crowded and there's something for climbers of all abilities. On top of that you've got long summers unspoilt by rain and some of the most stunning backdrops on earth.'

Climbing in Malta varies from technical boulder problems (performed a few feet off the ground without the aid of a rope) to an abundance of both sport climbs (clipping the rope into pre-placed rivets during ascent) and more dangerous trad climbs (fixing rope-supporting gear in cracks along the way). Most spectacular is the potential for deep water soloing – climbing without a rope over water deep enough to make the consequences of even a mighty fall little worse than a profound wedgie and a warm bath.

Many of Malta's finest climbs lie scattered along the south coast: the picturesque Blue Grotto is a popular haunt (Hello Boys is a fine route with a beautiful backdrop), while nearby Wied Babu is home to both sport routes (the powerful Kleen Kutter) and trad climbs (the long and fiddly Maltese Falcon). Over on Gozo, the dramatic rock arches of Wied Il-Mielah provide more laid-back beginners' lines.

Interested parties would do well to pick up a copy of *Malta Rock Climbing* by John Codling, Andrew Warrington and Richard Abela, published in 2007 and detailing 1,275 routes (337 in Gozo and 11 on Comino); the book is available for €28.50 from **www.malta-rockclimbing.com**, which is also a useful source of information on all things rock-related across the Maltese islands.

MALTA BY AREA

Level 22

dinners take in dishes such as pan-fried lamb marinated in honey and mint (from the West) and an exquisite Indonesian beef rendang with chillies, coconut milk and sublimely fragrant rice (from the East).

Shopping

Bay Street Complex
St George's Bay, St Julian's (2138 4422/www.baystreet.com.mt). **Open** 10am-10pm daily. **Map** p72 A2 ③⓪
Situated in Malta's entertainment district, this sprawling shopping complex houses big brand outlets like Mexx, Guess, French Connection, Marks & Spencer and the Pedigree Toyshop, plus sustenance from the Hard Rock Café, McDonald's, the Argentinian Steak House and countless other casual drinking and dining spots.

Cleland & Souchet
Block 14, Level 0, Portomaso, St Julian's (2138 9898/www.cleland souchet.com). **Open** 9am-7pm Mon-Sat. **Map** p72 B3 ③①
A two-floor domestic mecca selling contemporary homeware in a smart setting. The owners are true wine connoisseurs, and the upper floor houses

a huge selection of vintages that they also distribute to local restaurants. Cleland & Souchet regularly organises exhibitions by local artists, with displayed paintings for sale to the public.

De Fort Designerwear
15 Portomaso, St Julian's (2138 7687). **Open** 9am-7pm daily. **Map** p72 B3 ③②
Designer clothes in a designer setting, De Fort is an upmarket outlet in one of Malta's most exclusive locations. It carries clothing, swimwear and accessories for men and women from names such as Lacoste, Ralph Lauren, Polo Jeans and Moschino, with most of the stock boasting a suitably severe price tag. Fashion not for the faint-hearted.

Friction
Wilga Street, Paceville (2138 6748). **Open** *May-Sept* 9am-10pm Mon-Sat. *Oct-Apr* 9am-1pm, 4-7pm Mon-Sat. **Map** p72 B2 ③③
This colourful shop is a godsend to holidaymakers who forgot to pack that all-important item, with a great selection of surf-, beach- and streetwear, plus bags and other accessories including sunglasses and wallets by the likes of Mambo, Quiksilver and Colors of

California. An excellent balance of fashion and function, and popular with kids keen on the surfer look.

Porto

Portomaso Shopping Complex, St Julian's (2137 2079). **Open** 10am-7.30pm Mon-Sat; 10am-1pm Sun. **Map** p72 B3 ❸

A delightful shop selling stylish bags in casual and dressy lines by designer brands such as Francesco Biaisa, Ripani, Radley and Tula, plus stunning contemporary jewellery and accessories from the likes of Gaby's, Bulatti and Chartage. The helpful staff are clearly fond of every item on display.

Nightlife

Axis

St George's Road, Paceville (2135 8078/www.axis.com.mt). **Open** *June-Aug* 8pm-4am daily. *Sept-May* 8pm-4am Fri, Sat. **Admission** €4.08-€8.15. **Map** p72 A2 ❸

Axis has served as the beating heart of Paceville's clubbing scene since it introduced techno to Malta in the early 1990s. All musical tastes are catered for, with DJs taking crowds on a journey from commercial to more hard-edged electro as the night progresses, and with regular visits from the likes of Judge Jules, Sonique and members of the Ministry of Sound. Axis is also home to the Matrix VIP club – phone ahead to book a table.

BJ's Nightclub

Ball Street, Paceville (9949 3534). **Open** 10pm-4am daily. **Admission** free. **Map** p72 B2 ❸

BJ's is one of very few nightclubs in Malta offering live music every night, with a nice line in live jazz and regular improvised jam sessions. Its tucked away, subterranean location lends a uniquely intimate atmosphere, a million miles from the rush and bustle of more conventionally 'clubby' clubs. Every Easter, BJ's organises a music marathon for charity, assembling a host of local musicians who play continuously for 100 hours.

Fuego Salsa Bar

St George's Bay, St Julian's (2138 6746/www.fuego.com.mt). **Open** 8.30pm-2am Mon-Wed; 10pm-4am Thur-Sun. **Admission** free. **Map** p72 A2 ❸

Fuego fuses traditional Latin music with more commercial floor-filling sounds, and regularly draws crowds of music aficionados and fun-seeking tourists as a direct result. Visitors will find something to get their feet moving every night of the week, while those concerned about their form on the dancefloor can indulge in free salsa lessons (8.30-10.30pm Mon-Wed). **Other location** Qawra Coast, Qawra (2158 4933).

Havana

82 St George's Road, Paceville (2137 4500/www.havanamalta.com). **Open** 9pm-4am daily. **Admission** free. **Map** p72 A2 ❸

While the rest of the island goes mad for banging Balearic house, Havana doffs its baseball cap to more urban beats, with R&B top of the playlist and with hip hop and soul bringing up the rear. The venue comprises six bars spread across two floors and is almost always buzzing until the small hours.

Level 22

Level 22, Portomaso, St Julian's (2310 2222). **Open** 9.30pm-4am Wed-Sun. **Admission** free. **Map** p72 B3 ❸

This stunning club is set like a jewel on the 22nd floor of the posh Portomaso tower, with a strict entry policy – no shorts or scruffy clothes – and arresting ocean views lending the air of a Hollywood cast party. Crowds lean towards the older, hipper end of the clubbing spectrum, making good use of the comfortable leather sofas and suitably expensive drinks list in the early hours before strutting their stuff on the small dancefloor later on.

Qube

St Rita Street, Paceville (7999 4477/www.qubemalta.com). **Open** 8.30pm-4am daily. **Admission** free. **Map** p72 A2 ❹

MALTA BY AREA

Malta's only vodka bar serves a wide range of flavoured varieties from all over the world in both mixer and shooter form, with a suitably cheerful mix of upbeat house, R&B and even rock setting the dancefloor alight once the drinks have kicked in. Weekdays see regular themed nights of the '60s and school disco ilk, and the place is popular with international students.

Sabor

7 Wilga Street, Paceville (7942 9687). **Open** *June-Oct* 11pm-4am Wed, Fri, Sat. *Nov-May* 11pm-4am Fri, Sat. **Admission** free. **Map** p72 A2 ④①

Essentially one large dancefloor dominated by a central bar dispensing drinks to a mad-for-it crowd of locals and foreign students alike, Sabor does nothing to distinguish itself from the competition but seldom fails to please the punters with its affection for floor-filling house anthems its notorious 'anything goes' attitude.

Shadow Lounge

NEW *Hugo's Lounge, St George's Road, Paceville (2138 2264/www.hugoslounge malta.com).* **Open** varies. **Admission** free. **Map** p72 A2 ④②

A club that's trendier and more tranquil than most, drawing punters more interested in lounging than larging it to the uppermost floor of popular bar-restaurant Hugo's Lounge (p75), and with dancing and drinking in a glass-walled area with lovely views over the surrounding neighbourhood.

Sky Club

NEW *Westin Dragonara Resort, St Julian's (www.skyclubmalta.com).* **Open** times vary. **Admission** prices vary. **Map** p72 B2 ④③

This grand club, which constitutes the latest addition to the St Julian's nightlife scene, caters as much to corporate events as regular club nights – easily done, considering the fact that its VIP room alone has space for 700 people. It's still finding its feet, but house music is the name of the game and international DJs are already lining up to do their thing.

Styx

St George's Road, Paceville (2135 8078/www.axis.com.mt). **Open** *June-Aug* daily. *Sept-May* 11pm-4am Fri, Sat. **Admission** €4.08-€8.15. **Map** p72 A2 ④④

Venue of the moment, although seldom kicking before 2am, Styx is a revival of one of Malta's first clubs, now relocated above Axis and decked out with a truly cutting-edge, minimalist interior, a futuristic bar and a fancy VIP area. Wednesday and Friday nights are the big draws for electro and house fans.

Arts & leisure

Cynergi

St Augustine Street, St George's Bay, St Julian's (2371 0700/www.cynergi. com.mt). **Open** 6am-11pm daily. **Map** p72 A2 ④⑤

Malta's largest gym boasts over 100 cardio machines, an indoor pool, sauna, steam room and a range of professionally led classes. Membership options include monthly and student rates, and staff are happy to help orientate those not yet used to the wide variety of equipment on offer.

Dragonara Casino Barrière

Dragonara Palace, St Julian's (2138 2362/www.dragonara.com). **Open** *Sept-July* 10am-6am Mon-Thur; 24hrs Fri-Sun. *Aug* 24hrs daily. **Map** p72 C1 ④⑥

This is Malta's oldest casino, set in a grand 19th-century neo-classical palace and boasting a jaw-dropping range of slot machines, as well as entire rooms filled with blackjack, roulette, punto banco and poker gaming tables.

Eden Cinema

St Augustine Street, St George's Bay, St Julian's (2371 0400/www.eden cinemas.com.mt). **Open** according to screenings. **Map** p72 A2 ④⑦

Malta's largest cinema complex shows mainstream Hollywood releases in comfortable surroundings. The complex is also home to the 20-lane Eden Superbowl, Malta's only bowling alley (2371 0777, www.edensuperbowl.com, open 10am-midnight daily).

MALTA BY AREA

Vittoriosa Waterfront

The Three Cities & Around

Vittoriosa, Senglea and Cospicua – or Birgu, Isla and Bormla in the native Maltese – are medieval towns that straddle two peninsulas jutting out into the Grand Harbour. Vittoriosa, nestled in the shadow of impregnable **Fort St Angelo**, is both the oldest of the Three Cities and the richest in historical sights, with the parish **St Lawrence Church**, devastated by fire in 1532 and subsequently rebuilt, among its most important early buildings.

It was with the coming of the Knights of St John, however, that the city came into its own, selected as their seat and quickly becoming the site of numerous palaces and churches. The main street – today's Main Gate Street – divided the town in two both physically and socially: the western area or *fuori collachio* was once inhabited by locals; the eastern area or *collachio*, marked off by a few simple stone bollards, was home to the Knights'

exclusive residences (now privately owned but still worthy of a stroll).

Following the grand rebuilding of Vittoriosa, the Knights further insured against foreign invasion by founding two new fortified towns, Senglea and Cospicua. When the Ottomans invaded in the Great Siege of 1565, Cospicua was almost completely largely destroyed, but Senglea and Vittoriosa withstood fierce repetitive assaults. The settlements were subsequently further fortified by two sets of semicircular walls: the Margarita Lines and the longer Cottonera Lines, which, at almost eight kilometres (five miles) are the longest walls ever built in Malta. Senglea and Cospicua today provide very little in the way of attractions save the former's **Our Lady of Victories Church** and **Gardjola Garden**, an attractive public space offering great views of the Grand Harbour.

Recent years have seen heavy investment in the cities, especially Vittoriosa. By far and away the largest project is the rehabilitation of Vittoriosa's Waterfront, with many grand upgrades to the lovely seafront buildings – among them the smart **Casino di Venezia** and the **Maritime Museum**.

There are also several attractions in the surrounding region vying for the attention of visitors, including **Fort Rinella** and two fascinating ancient sites, the burial chambers of **Hal Saflieni Hypogeum** and **Tarxien Temples**, both in Paola.

Sights & museums

Fort Rinella

St Rocco Road, Kalkara (2180 0992/ www.wirtartna.org). **Open** 10am-5pm daily. *Tours* on the hr. *Animated tours* 2.30pm. **Admission** €6.99; €3.49-€5.82 reductions. *Animated tours* €4.66 extra. **Map** p85 D1 ●

A few kilometres north of Vittoriosa, Fort Rinella is the most important military relic from the British era. The fort was erected in the 1870s specifically to house the Armstrong 100-ton gun, the single largest gun ever made. The Armstrong's shells were capable of piercing the steel hulls of ships and so it was mounted here to protect the entrance to the Grand Harbour. It's worth timing your visit to coincide with the daily re-enactments of everyday life in the old fort.

Fort St Angelo

The Waterfront, Vittoriosa (2295 4300). **Open** no fixed times. **Admission** free. **Map** p85 C1 ●

A fort has stood on this site since the end of the 12th century, but this present incarnation dates back to the arrival of the Knights in 1530, who enlarged and strengthened the foundations of the original structure. The building fell into disuse following World War II despite suffering only superficial damage, and is currently undergoing a rehabilitation project.

MALTA BY AREA

Senglea Point

Save Haven Gardens

Vedete

TRIQ IL-BRIGIEL

TRIQ IX-XATT

St Philip

TRIQ IL-FWWO-MINI

TRIQ ID-DEJRNA

TRIQ IL-PWVA

TRIQ IL-VICTORIA

TRIQ IS-SUR

TRIQ IL-PONTA

MISHRA 1-4 TA'SETTEMBRI

TRIQ IL-GILJAN

TRIQ IL-KBIRA

TRIQ IS-SUR

Id-Dahla Tal-Francizi

● Sights & museums
● Eating & drinking
● Shopping
● Nightlife
● Arts & leisure

The Three Cities

C **D** **E**

Chapel of St Anne

Fort St Angelo

Angelo Wharf

Porta Della Marina

Kalkara Creek

Bighi Salla Port

Dockyard Creek

Birgu Marina

Poste d'Allemagne

TRIQ IL-MIRATUR

TRIQ IL-HABS L-ANTIK

TRIQ SAN LAWRENZ

XATT IL-FORN

Casino di Venezia

Sacra Infermeria

TRIQ HILDA TABONE

Poste de Castille

Maritime Museum

Inquisitor's Palace

Armerija

San Lawrenz

Freedom Monument

Connor Gate

TRIQ TA XAGHRA

MINA IX-XATT

TRIQ SAN PAWL

TRIQ PIETRU U SAN PAWL

Dockyard Terrace

TRIQ IT-TARZNA

Poste de Provence

Madonna Ta Vitorja

Il-Macina

TRIQ SAN LAWRENZ

Poste d'Aragon

TRIQ SANT'IWARDU

Poste de France

Poste d'Italie

Fort St Michael

Cottonera Marina

TRIQ SAN LAWRENZ

0   300 m

0   300 yds

© Copyright Time Out Group 2008

Senglea p83

The upper Magisterial Palace and St Anne's Chapel remain the property of the Order and are not open to the public, but visitors are welcome to wander the lower open-air grounds, and may also gain access to the (usually closed) central courtyard if someone happens to be there to let them in.

Hal Saflieni Hypogeum
Cemetary Street, Paola (2180 5019/ www.heritagemalta.org). **Open** *Tours* 9am-4pm on the hr. **Admission** €9.32; €4.66 reductions. **Map** p85 D5 ❸
Uncovered by accident during routine building work in 1902, this sprawling necropolis is believed to date back to as far as 3600 BC, and throughout history may have served as the site for over 7,000 burials. These twisting corridors and haunting chambers were closed for several years after it was revealed that carbon dioxide exhaled by visitors was damaging the limestone walls. Since reopening, just 80 people are allowed in per day in on-the-hour tours, and booking in advance – either at the National Museum of Archaeology (p55), or via the Heritage Malta website – is essential.

Inquisitor's Palace
Main Gate Street, Vittoriosa (2182 7006/www.heritagemalta.org). **Open** 9am-5pm daily. **Admission** €4.66; €1.16-€2.33 reductions. **Map** p85 D3 ❹
Despite serving as the seat of Malta's Inquisition from its formation in 1574 to its dissolution in 1798, the most interesting features of this large Baroque building actually pre-date the Inquisition, and include a small cloistered courtyard with a cross-vaulted Gothic ceiling built upon the Knights' arrival. The prison cells provide a cramped and suitably dank diversion on the way to the upper floor, home to the Chancery and the Waiting Room – both decorated with Baroque friezes and the coats of arms of the Inquisitors who served in Malta – as well as a chilling Tribunal Room, home to a wooden throne on which it's only too easy to imagine a member of the Inquisition.

Malta At War Museum
Courvre Porte, Vittoriosa (2180 0992/www.wirtartna.org). **Open** 10am-4pm Mon-Sat. *Tours* 11.30am, 2.30pm. **Admission** €3.49; €1.16-€2.33 reductions. **Map** p85 D4 ❺
Under a deluge of bombs, the residents of the Three Cities cowered, sometimes for weeks on end, in a claustrophobic warren of underground tunnels and honeycomb rooms gouged deep into the bedrock beneath the landward fortifications of Vittoriosa. Today these underground shelters have been furnished with period props and original artefacts, with convincing re-creations of the communal dormitory, private cubicles, birthing room and wardens' office, and with a separate exhibition offering a fascinating (if sometimes grim) insight into wartime life. There are also screenings of a film about the Maltese resistance made in 1943 to bolster the nation's morale at the height of the campaign to bomb it into surrender.

Maritime Museum
The Waterfront, Vittoriosa (2166 0052/www.heritagemalta.org). **Open** 9am-5pm daily. **Admission** €4.66; €1.16-€2.33 reductions. **Map** p85 C3 ❻
A masterpiece of industrial architecture, the Maritime Museum is located in the former bakery of the occupying British forces and serves to illustrate man's naval and maritime activities in and around the Maltese islands. The exhibits range from anchors and amphorae salvaged from Roman shipwrecks and early navigational contraptions to models and prints of various vessels throughout the ages, with the entire engine of a steam ship a notable highlight. There is also a large section dedicated to the oceanic exploits of the Knights, with models of several of their boats including an 18th-century galley.

Our Lady of Victories Church
Pope Benedict XV Square, Senglea (2182 7203). **Open** 6.15-11.30am, 4-6pm Mon-Sat; 7-11.30am, 5-6.30pm Sun. **Admission** free. **Map** p85 B4 ❼

MALTA BY AREA

The hard sell

Maltese brands stand firm in a landslide of EU imports.

Bajtra

With a wine exporter like Italy next door, most diminutive nations would have long ago called it a day and thrown in the grapes along with the towel. Yet small Maltese producers have used EU membership – and the inevitable flood of imports that followed – as an opportunity to push home the fact that Maltese wines can be as good as imports, if not better.

Getting the Maltese to become loyal to local labels hasn't been easy – colonised many time over, this is a nation with an ingrained preference for purchasing foreign products – but marketing execs at local wineries are finally noting an increase in sales of quality Maltese wines. These include **Gran Cavalier** merlots and syrahs, chardonnays and champagnes by **Marsovin** and also a rosé from **Medina Vineyards**.

Nor is it just wines that you should be keeping an eye out for. Maltese olive oil is also an increasingly big business thanks to the **Savina** brand, and the industry is now due a boost in production as a result of PRIMO (Project for the Revival of the Indigenous Maltese Olive), which encourages locals to plant their own indigenous Bidnija olive trees and press their own oil. Then there's the popular **Kinnie** soft drink – a blend of oranges and aromatic herbs dating back to the early 1950s – and a range of Maltese liqueurs including **Bajtra**, **Limuncell** (made from Gozo lemons) and **Zeppi**, the latter coming in several familiar island flavours such as anisette, honey and pomegranate.

Yet no Maltese product has quite ingrained itself upon the national psyche like the distinct yellow can of the ubiquitous **Cisk** beer, an international prizewinner for Farsons brewery (which also produces the more toothsome **Hopleaf** ale). With sales unaffected by a rash of cheap EU-related imports, Cisk has shown that Maltese producers can play the game and beat the big guys, and now there are plenty of others lining up to do likewise.

Named after the victory of the Great Siege, Senglea's original parish church was destroyed in World War II before being rebuilt in a larger but less ornate form. Its imposing façade and elegant dome are visible from afar, while the interior is home to a grand baldacchino over the main altar. The church's main attraction is the reputedly miraculous statue of *Kristu Redentur* in the chapel adjacent to the chancel, a stirring rendition of the bloodied Christ lumbering beneath the cross.

St Lawrence Church

The Waterfront, Vittoriosa (no phone). **Open** 9.30am-noon, 4.30-5.30pm Mon-Sat; 9.30-10.30am, 4.30-5.30pm Sun. **Admission** free. **Map** p85 C3 ⑧

A church has existed in some form on this same site since the 12th century, although the present edifice was designed in 1681 by Lorenzo Gafa, a master of architectural composition. It was the Knights' conventual church during their stay in Vittoriosa and still contains many of their riches, displayed during the feast of the patron saint on 10 August each year. The church is also home to a fine painting of St Lawrence's martyrdom by the Italian Baroque master Mattia Preti.

Tarxien Temples

Neolithic Temples Street, Paola (2169 5578/www.heritagemalta.org). **Open** 9am-5pm daily. **Admission** €2.33; free-€1.25 reductions. **Map** p85 D5 ⑨

First discovered in 1914 by famers who unexpectedly hit stone while ploughing a field, the Neolithic temples of Tarxien are among the most intricate and intriguing historical sites on the islands. A short walk from the Hal Saflieni Hypogeum (and similarly dating back as far as 3600 BC), the temples are most noteworthy for their fascinatingly detailed rock carvings of domestic and farm animals

Eating & drinking

L'Angolo di Vino

NEW *Mistral Street, Vittoriosa (9904 5857).* **Open** 8.30pm-1am Wed-Sun. **Bar**. **Map** p85 D3 ⑩

A business venture from the nose of noted Maltese broadcast journalist Glenn Bedingfield, this cavernous bar is one of the most reliable when it comes to selecting local and international vintages. Customers range from wine boffins to complete beginners, all of whom are taken under the wing of the welcoming, well-informed staff.

Del Borgo p90

Del Borgo

*36 Tower of St John Street, Vittoriosa
(2180 3710).* **Open** *June-Oct* 7.30pm-
1am daily. *Sept-May* 7.30pm-1am Mon-
Sat; 11.30am-2.30pm, 7.30pm-1am Sun.
Bar. Map p85 D4 ⑪
With an 18th-century cellar setting
embellished by the most tasteful modern design, Del Borgo continues to dish
out exquisite food, excellent service
and an extensive wine list. Bar food
ranges from platters to pasta and a list
of changing specials, all of it washed
down with a fine bottle of white or red
decanted at your table.

Il-Forn

*26 North Street, Vittoriosa (2182
0379/www.birgu.com).* **Open** 7.30pm-
1am Tue-Sun. **Bar**. Map p85 D3 ⑫
Three well-sized millrooms, two court-
yards and a handful of smaller rooms
comprise this enormous wine bar – the
area's first – located in a former bakery tucked away in the Collachio and
owned by an Austrian artist whose
colourful paintings adorn the walls.
The extensive wine list covers more
than 80 foreign and local wines.

Ristorante Venezia

*Casino di Venezia, Scamps Palace,
The Waterfront, Vittoriosa (2397
9131).* **Open** 7.30-11.30pm Mon, Wed-
Sun. **€€€**. **Italian**. Map p85 C3 ⑬
Fine Italian dining on a wide terrace
with sweeping views over towards
Senglea and the Grand Harbour.
Starters might include a stunning lin-
guine rizzi (tossed with garlic, fresh
herbs and sea urchins), while mains
offer the likes of subtly spiced rack of
lamb and an abundance of fresh fish.
Those under 18 will be refused entry
due to the restaurant's casino location.

Tate Café Bar

*Vault 1, Old Treasury Building,
The Waterfront, Vittoriosa (2180
8828).* **Open** 9am-midnight daily.
Vegetarian. Map p85 C3 ⑭
The Tate's diminutive interior is more
than made up for by a large outdoor
area decked with stylish chairs and
offering great views over the marina.

It's the perfect place to chill out over a
cup of coffee or a glass of wine, with a
wide range of generously portioned,
genuinely delicious vegetarian food –
from platters to pizza and pasta. In fact,
the Tate is the first restaurant in Malta
in which meat (including fish) is completely off the menu.

Two and a Half Lemon

NEW *Vault 5, Old Treasury Building,
The Waterfront, Vittoriosa (2180
9909/www.twoandahalflemon.com).*
Open noon-3pm, 7.30-11pm daily.
€€€. **Mediterranean**. Map p85 C3 ⑮
You've got to try the black rock grill at
this hip new restaurant by the water's
edge: a fillet of beef or tuna steak
cooked to perfection on a hot slab at
your table. Meanwhile, less adventurous diners are catered for with conventional dishes such as grilled sea bream,
charred chicken breast and braised
lamb shank. Artistic touches blend
seamlessly with the traditional Maltese
tile motif and old stone walls of this historic treasury building.

Arts & leisure

Casino Di Venezia

*Scamps Palace, The Waterfront,
Vittoriosa (2180 5580).* **Open** *Slot
machines* 2pm-2am Mon-Thur; 2pm-
5am Fri, Sat; noon-4am Sun. *Gaming
tables* 3pm-2am Mon-Thur; 3pm-5am
Fri, Sat; 3pm-4am Sun. Map p85 C3 ⑯
Sister of the Casino di Venezia in
Venice, this sumptuous gaming centre
is housed in the stunning former headquarters of the Knights' naval fleet.
There are rows of slot machines as well
as a lobby bar on the ground floor, with
rooms of gaming tables upstairs.

Marsa Sports Club

*Aldo Moro Street, Marsa (2123 3851/
www.marsasportsclub.com).* **Open** 8am-
10.30pm daily. Map p85 C5 ⑰
This privately owned sports club
offers 19 all-weather tennis courts, five
squash courts, an 18-hole, par-68 golf
course, a large open-air swimming
pool, a cricket pitch and a polo club.
Tournaments run throughout the year.

Sliema

Once a sleepy seaside town lined with elegant Baroque houses, the Sliema of today is a bustling coastal resort, its once tranquil coast teeming with blocks of expensive apartments and its commercial centre packed with offices, high street shops, hotels, restaurants and bars.

The town centre itself has no noteworthy historical sights to speak of, but enjoys a unique upmarket buzz thanks to the relative affluence of its inhabitants, a high concentration of tourists and a constant influx of islanders commuting in to make the most of the abundant amenities. Come summer, Sliema also serves as a temporary home to the large number of foreign students studying English at numerous language schools in the area.

Sliema takes its name from the Maltese word *sliem*, meaning 'peace' – appropriate during its 19th-century foundation (it was originally settled to provide an upper-class coastal retreat for British rulers and Maltese nobles), but far less so today. In recent decades Sliema has undergone a dramatic shift both aesthetically and in terms of its social fabric, with the majority of its early villas demolished to make way for high-rise apartment blocks, most of them spacious, luxurious and extremely expensive (an address on Tower Road remains one of Malta's most prestigious).

The commercial hub is largely concentrated around the Sliema Ferries area, Bisazza Street and Tower Road, with the latter bearing left when it reaches the northern

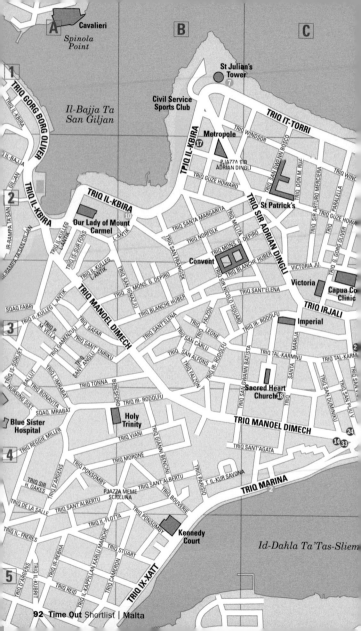

A Cavalieri
Spinola Point

B

C

1

TRIQ GORG BORG OLIVER

TRIQ IL-BAJJA

TRIQ IL-BAJJA SAN GILJAN

*Il-Bajja Ta
San Giljan*

St Julian's
Tower ⑦

Civil Service
Sports Club

TRIQ IL-KBIRA

Metropole ⑰

TRIQ IT-TORRI

TRIQ WINDSOR

PJAZZA SIR
ADRIAN DINGLI

TRIQ SAN GWANN BOSCO

TRIQ DON M. RUZ

TRIQ WINI

TRIQ SIR ARTURO MERCIECA

TRIQ GUZE HOWA

TRIQ GUZE HOWARD

2

TRIQ IL-KBIRA

IR-RAMPA TA'SAN

RAMPA TA'SAN GILJAN

TRIQ IL-KBIRA

Our Lady of Mount
Carmel ⑩

TRIQ IL-KULLEG
L'ANTIK

TRIQ IS-SIR FONS

TRIQ IL-KULLEG L'ANTIK

TRIQ SAN FRANGISK

TRIQ MONS. G. DEPIRO

TRIQ SAN IGNAZJU

TRIQ SANTA MARGARITA

TRIQ NORFOLK

TRIQ MELITA

TRIQ MONS. G. DEPIRO

Convent

TRIQ BLANCHE HUBER

TRIQ SIR NICOLO ISOUARD

TRIQ BLANCHE HUBER

TRIQ SANT'ELENA

St Patrick's

TRIQ SIR ADRIAN DINGLI

Victoria

Capua Co
Clinic

VICTORIA JU

TRIQ SANT'ELENA

TRIQ G. BORG OLIVER

TRIQ IRJALI

3

TRIQ IS-SQIRLET

TRIQ IL-KULLEG L'ANTIK

SQAQ FABRI

TRIQ P. M. VELLA

TRIQ A. GAFAR

TRIQ GAMENZJU

TRIQ SANT'ENRIKU

BALLUT

TRIQ BONAVITA

TRIQ IMRABAT

TRIQ SANT'ANGLU

TRIQ TONNA

TRIQ FALZON

TRIQ SAN LEONE

TRIQ SAN CARLU

TRIQ SAN ALFONS

TRIQ FALZON

TRIQ IR- RODOLFU

Imperial

TRIQ IR. RODOLFU

TRIQ TAL-KARMNU

SANTA MARIJA

TRIQ TAL-KARM

TRIQ SAN PAUV

TRIQ MANOEL DIMECH

TRIQ SAN GWANN BATISTA

Sacred Heart
Church ⑲

TRIQ SAN DUMINKU

4

NURSING SIST

SQAQ. MRABAT

Blue Sister
Hospital

TRIQ REGGIE MILLER

TRIQ SIR
H. OAKES

TRIQ D'ARGENS

TRIQ PONSOMBY

TRIQ DE LA SALLE

TRIQ SANT'ALBERTU

TRIQ IR- RODOLFU

Holy
Trinity

TRIQ VIANI

TRIQ MORONE

TRIQ GJANN BENCINI

TRIQ SANT'ALBERTU

T. IL-KUR SAVONA

TRIQ PARISIO

TRIQ BOUVERIE

PJAZZA MEME
SCICLUNA

TRIQ MANOEL DIMECH

TRIQ SANT'AGATA

TRIQ MARINA

⑭ ㉝

Id-Dahla Ta'Tas-Sliem

5

TRIQ D'ARGENS

TRIQ IL-KUBRIT

TRIQ IL- FRERES

TRIQ IR-REBJA

TRIQ REID

TRIQ IL-FLOTTA

TRIQ KAPPILLAN KARLU MANCHE

TRIQ STUART

TRIQ CAMERON

TRIQ PONSOMBY

Kennedy
Court

TRIQ IX-XATT

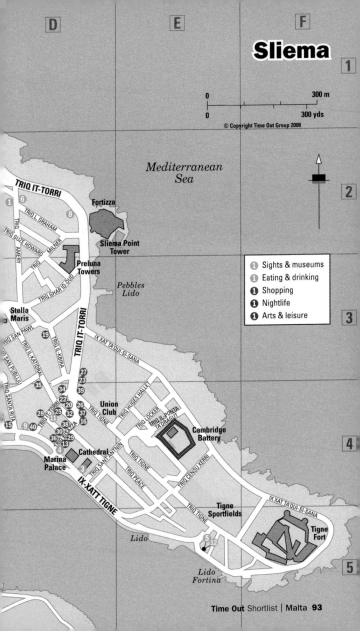

Sliema

Mediterranean Sea

D **E** **F**

1

0   300 m
0   300 yds
© Copyright Time Out Group 2008

2

TRIQ IT-TORRI

Fortizza

Sliema Point Tower

Preluna Towers

Pebbles Lido

① Sights & museums
① Eating & drinking
① Shopping
① Nightlife
① Arts & leisure

3

Stella Maris

TRIQ IT-TORRI

IX-XATT TA' QUI-SI-SANA

Union Club

TRIQ TIGNE

TRIQ HUGES HALLET

TRIQ LOCKER

TRIQ IL-PONTA TA' DRAGUT

Cambridge Battery

Cathedral

Marina Palace

IX-XATT TIGNE

TRIQ SANT ANTNIN

TRIQ TIGNE

TRIQ PEACE

TRIQ CENSU XERRI

TRIQ TIGNE

IX-XATT TA' QUI-SI-SANA

4

Tigne Sportfields

Tigne Fort

Lido

Lido Fortina

5

b'art

shore before turning into a long, wide promenade perched above a strip of rocky coastline with lovely views of the Mediterranean. It's affectionately known as 'the Front' by locals, who use it for the daily ritual of the *passiggata* – a leisurely early evening stroll. The rocky shelf also fills with bathers in the summer, and makes a convenient swimming spot for those less likely to trek to the northwest coast.

Eating & drinking

b'art

Amery Street (2133 3333/www.bart malta.com). **Open** 4-7pm Mon-Thur; 4.30pm-midnight Fri; 6-11pm Sat. **Bar**. Map p93 D2 ❶

The brainchild of Stefan Borg Manduca, b'art is both a bar and a celebration of contemporary art. Not that it's an art gallery per se: artists are invited to display their pieces to visually alter and enhance the stylish venue, and the onus on staff is more about blending cocktails and serving a variety of fine wines than knowing their Matisse from their Mondrian. The attracts an interesting mix of executives, academics, artists and collectors.

Black Gold

The Strand (2133 4808). **Open** 9am-1am daily. **Bar**. Map p92 C4 ❷

An established bar drawing a regular crop of sailors who work in the local harbour, as well as a motley mix of Sliema residents and out-of-towners looking for a more authentic dive in which to wet their whistle. The atmosphere is friendly and informal and the music is classic rock. In summer the mirrored interior is exchanged for alfresco tables with an oceanside view.

Café Bottega

Tigné Seafront (2133 6461). **Open** 9am-1am daily. **Café**. Map p93 D4 ❸

Baguettes, pizzas, plates of pasta and desserts including own-made cheesecakes and pastries are all served at this delightful café, perfectly located to offer a break from bustling Sliema and with an on-site store selling handmade jewellery if you're looking for quality souvenirs. Choose between the comfortable modern interior or the shaded outdoor terrace with splendid views of Valletta. Evenings bring the mellow accompaniment of a live guitarist or violinist and you can also purchase the works of a talented artist who occasionally paints on site.

Café Giorgio

17 Tigné Seafront (2134 2456). **Open** *Apr-Oct* 8am-midnight daily. *Nov-Mar* 8am-10pm daily. **Café**. **Map** p93 D4 ❹

Members of Sliema's younger generation love to pose and people-watch at this popular corner café, with its outdoor tables spilling on to the pavements at the bottom of a busy shopping strip. The brass and wood interior of Café Giorgio has remained unchanged for time out of mind, as has the homely menu of hearty pastries and cakes, with notable highlights including *pastizzi* (filo pockets with a ricotta or pea filling) and a gorgeous chocolate gateau. Some of the tables enjoy superb sea views.

Can Thai

Fortina Spa Resort, Tigné Seafront (2346 6666). **Open** 12.30-2.30pm, 7-10.30pm Mon, Tue-Thur. €€€. **Asian**. **Map** p93 E5 ❺

An upmarket eaterie serving an intoxicating fusion of Cantonese and Thai cuisines, listed separately on a menu that allows customers to mix and match as the fancy takes them: duck spring rolls followed by green prawn curry, for example, or Thai fishcakes followed by sweet and sour chicken. If you're having difficulty choosing, there's a set menu offering the best of everything for €22.13 per head. On balmy summer evenings, be sure to dine on the outdoor terrace in the restaurant's relaxing tropical garden, but do book well in advance.

La Cuccagna

47 Amery Street (2134 6703). **Open** noon-2.30pm, 7pm-midnight Tue-Sun. €€. **Mediterranean**. **Map** p93 D2 ❻

Tucked just off the Sliema seafront, this small, traditional townhouse has been converted into a successful eaterie with an informal atmosphere more akin to a typical Maltese home than a restaurant. Cuccagna is best known for its delicious pizzas, with thin crusts and fresh toppings as standard: try the version with rocket, parmesan and parma ham. Service is excellent, the staff smiling and attentive and the atmosphere always upbeat, but book ahead or be there before 8pm to ensure you don't miss out.

Exiles

Tower Road (2134 0909). **Open** *May-Oct* noon-2am daily. **Bar**. **Map** p92 B1 ❼

Café Bottega

MALTA BY AREA

Exiles is a rough-and-ready beach bar on the rocky Sliema seashore that boasts a laid-back atmosphere and easy-living attitude throughout its summer opening. By day, the snack bar caters for those lounging at the public beach, while at sunset the smell of barbecued food fills the air along with chilled reggae grooves from the in-house sound system. It may be basic in the extreme, but there are few places to be found offering such an authentic Mediterranean summer vibe.

Mojito

NEW *Europa Hotel, 138 Tower Road (2133 4070).* **Open** 7pm-3am daily. **Bar**. Map p93 D2 ❽

Mojito is a stylish new bar enjoying a privileged position opposite the Sliema seafront and a smart location within the Europa Hotel. Originally a lounge bar, Mojito has recently been transformed into a bright and vibrant meeting place with a clubby atmosphere and a DJ mixing R&B, Latin music and upbeat electronic dance tunes to a more mature crowd of local and imported hipsters. As the name suggests, this is also a great place to come for cocktails galore, expertly mixed from a list as long as the bartender's arm.

Offshore

4 The Strand (no phone). **Open** 7.30am-11pm daily. **Café**. Map p93 D4 ❾

A perennially popular café that serves as something of a poser's paradise for the crowd of happening Sliema youngsters who flock here night and day, interrupting their social agenda only to nod attentively to the tasteful music or nibble on one of the expertly made (if rather expensive) baguettes, focaccias or filled tortillas.

Snoopy's

265 Tower Road (2134 5466). **Open** noon-3pm, 7-10.30pm Mon, Wed-Fri; 10am-3pm, 7-10.30pm Sat, Sun. €€€. **Fusion**. Map p92 B2 ❿

Malta's answer to the British gastropub, Snoopy's has remained in the hands of the same devoted family for over three decades, and while a recent refurbishment may have introduced an element of sophistication, nothing seems able to erode its old-fashioned charm. The beautifully presented food is a fusion of European and oriental cuisines, with generous fillet steaks and outstanding pasta dishes for those seeking something a little more conventional. The weekend breakfast menu is also a winner, satisfying even the heartiest of appetites.

Ta' Kris

80 Fawwara Lane (2133 7367). **Open** noon-3.30pm, 6.30-11.30pm daily. €€. **Maltese**. Map p93 D4 ⓫

Those looking for traditional Maltese food in an authentic environment need look no further. Ta' Kris was once a local bakery – the large oven is still visible from the entrance and certain old tools adorn the yellow walls and ceiling – but it now serves established seasonal specials along the lines of broccoli or marrow soup, vegetable and tuna risotto, rabbit stew and the customary bragjoli (beef olives) in a tomato and wine sauce. The location also makes for a convenient break on any local shopping spree.

Taste

Fortina Spa Resort, Tigné Seafront (2346 6666). **Open** 12.30-2.30pm, 7-10pm Tue-Sun. €€€. **Fusion**. Map p93 E5 ⓬

Vietnamese cooking is fused with Mediterranean flavours at this popular seafront restaurant, with a menu of exquisite and well-presented dishes originally created by British chef Tom Kime, an erstwhile colleague of Jamie Oliver's (he actually cooked for Oliver's wedding). The open kitchen, with its colourful mosaic backdrop, makes for a visual highlight, but it's the food coming out of it that really seals the deal: the fennel-crusted blue fin tuna and the harissa spiced rack of lamb from the Mediterranean menu are outstanding, while a range of colourful Vietnamese options include the likes of cinnamon-marinated duck breast and a subtly aromatic prawn curry.

MALTA BY AREA

Wings of change

The people helping Malta remain a birdwatcher's paradise.

Malta's position on the migratory route between Europe and Africa makes it the perfect spot to catch sight of our feathered friends in flight – provided the hunters don't get them first.

Few pastimes are as deeply ingrained in the Maltese psyche as shooting birds, with the evening calm here regularly broken by the crack of a shotgun: turtledoves and quail are the main targets, although locals will happily take aim at pretty much anything streaking across the sky.

Legislation in 1980 introduced a clearly defined hunting season and a range of areas and species off limits to shooters, but the rules are regularly flouted without any punishment handed down – as a group numbering between 16 and 17,000, Maltese hunters and trappers constitute one demographic that the politicians are keen to keep onside.

As such, it's been left largely to the devoted conservationists at **Birdlife Malta** (2134 7644, www.birdlifemalta.org) to keep an eye on proceedings, and with more than 3,000 members (and the Birdlife Global Partnership's claim to more than 2.5 million members worldwide), they're clearly more than just a niggling thorn in the side of the shooters.

'We're not trying to get hunting banned altogether,' says Dr André Raine, conservation manager at Birdlife Malta. 'Hunting in some form will always be legal here, as it is in all countries. What we're pushing for is an end to illegal spring hunting and the hunting of protected species.'

As such, Birdlife Malta spent April 2008 ensconced in a vigilant Spring Watch Camp that brought them face to face with illegal hunters across the islands, and which left them on the receiving end of much vandalism or verbal abuse. Despite this, volunteers from across the world are still flocking to help out, and the organisation is happy to pair concerned parties with activities ranging from ringing and counting birds to satellite tracking their migratory progress and planting trees. It's the perfect trip for tourists of a different feather.

Shopping

Accessorize/Monsoon

2-3 Bisazza Street (2131 7951). **Open** 9.30am-7pm Mon-Fri; 9.30am-7.30pm Sat. **Map** p93 D4 ⑬

Accessorize offers every kind of accessory imaginable, from bags and purses to jewellery, belts, hats, gloves and cosmetics. The adjoining Monsoon outlet – the two shops are interconnected and run by the same people – provides a colourful selection of evening dresses, as well as an eclectic mix of stylish and affordable casual clothes.
Other location Accessorize, Embassy Complex, Santa Lucia Street, Valletta (2125 2134).

Bejewelled

3 Manuel Dimech Street (2134 6757). **Open** 9.30am-1.30pm, 4-7pm Mon-Sat. **Map** p92 C4 ⑭

A tiny outlet that stands out from the crowd for its mix of well-crafted jewellery tailored to dress up any outfit – from chunky contemporary pieces to more classic gold and silver perfect for complementing formal eveningwear.

BHS

9 The Strand (2131 0811/www. camillerigroup.com). **Open** 9am-1.30pm, 4-7.30pm Mon-Fri; 9am-2pm, 4-8pm Sat. **Map** p93 D4 ⑮

BHS offers a trusted line of more conservative clothing for men, women and children. This two-storey shop also has a section dedicated to stylish homeware, with a range of bed linen, bathroom accessories and kitchen utensils on offer at affordable prices.
Other location 195-196 Merchant Street, Valletta (2124 1633).

Books Plus

Bisazza Street (2133 9400). **Open** 9.30am-7pm Mon-Sat. **Map** p93 D4 ⑯

A friendly, informal bookstore set on two floors and offering the usual bestsellers, general interest reads and a healthy selection of books on Maltese history and culture, as well as a range of specialist titles that tend to be unavailable elsewhere on the islands.

Brilliant

NEW *230 Tower Road (2131 7387).* **Open** 10am-6pm Mon-Sat. **Map** p92 B2 ⑰

The shop window of this designer light specialist is a real head turner, with a range of outrageous lampshades glimmering behind the glass. Each piece at the aptly named Brilliant – from baroque chandeliers to minimalist steel floor lamps – is a work of art in itself and proudly displayed as it would be in a gallery, with stock culled from designer houses such as Moooi, Flos and Foscarini. The interior design of the store itself is as luminous and disarming as the swankiest of its lamps.

Carmelo Micallef Bakery

2 St Trophimus Street (2134 0628). **Open** 10am-7pm daily. **Map** p92 C4 ⑱

Beyond the church, there are few totems around which Maltese society gravitates quite so reverently as its local bakeries, and this is one of the oldest and most respected, turning out a range of the best breads and pastries on the islands on a daily basis, and the perfect place to stock up on materials for a picnic on the Sliema seafront.

Casa Natura

117 High Street (2131 9929). **Open** 9am-1.30pm, 4.30-8pm Mon-Sat. **Map** p93 D3 ⑲

One of the few stores in Malta catering to the health-conscious, Casa Natura is well stocked with jars of vitamins and minerals, herbal teas, organic products and items for those suffering from all manner of allergies or health conditions, not to mention vegan foods and ingredients. Staff are well informed and happy to offer advice.

Cescas

Bisazza Street (2133 1041). **Open** 9.30am-1.30pm, 4.30-7pm Mon-Fri; 9.30am-7.30pm Sat. **Map** p93 D4 ⑳

The perfect place to shop for a classy pair of shoes, boots or sandals for men or women, with a small selection of matching bags also in stock. Prices may be slightly higher than at other local outlets, but the quality of the

MALTA BY AREA

products on offer is never in doubt, and the store has a reputation for friendly, well-informed staff providing top-notch customer care.

Other location Embassy Complex, Santa Lucia Street, Valletta (2122 5791).

Eighteen-Ninety by Camilleri Paris Mode

Annunciation Square (2134 4838/ www.camilleriparismode.com). **Open** 4.30-7.30pm Mon; 9.30am-7.30pm Tue-Fri; 9.30am-1pm, 4.30-6.30pm Sat. **Map** p92 C3 **㉑**

A family-run shop that prides itself on being one of the island's most respected retailers of all things domestic and design-related, including tableware, luxury towels, bed linen, lighting, carpeting and a range of contemporary and antique furniture. There's also a selection of fine food and wines, crystal glasses, wedding gowns, lifestyle products and exclusive fabrics. Prices are high but quality and cutting-edge designs come as standard.

Est Est Est

68 Tower Road (2132 0160/www.est-est-est.com). **Open** 9am-1pm, 4-7pm Mon-Sat. **Map** p93 D4 **㉒**

A godsend for dinner guests short on gift ideas, Est Est Est offers speciality foods ranging from own-made marmalades to exquisite chocolates and sumptuous terrines. The shop also stocks a wide selection of champagnes, wines and liqueurs, all of which staff will happily wrap, and there are hampers and free home deliveries for those seeking a gift with added gusto (or, more importantly, just an indulgent treat for themselves).

Evans

Tower Road (2132 3386/www.evans. ltd.uk). **Open** 9.30am-7pm Mon-Fri; 9.30am-7.30pm Sat. **Map** p93 D3 **㉓**

Home to a selection of clothing to flatter women from size 16 and up, the Maltese branch of this popular British franchise stocks everything from dresses to denim, knitwear, suits and shoes, all of it supremely easy on the eyes and eminently affordable.

Brilliant

Eighteen-Ninety by
Camilleri Paris Mode p99

Exotique

*380 Manuel Dimech Street (2133 1775/
www.exotique.com.mt).* **Open** 9.30am-
1.30pm, 4-7.30pm Mon-Fri; 9.30am-
1.30pm, 4-8pm Sat. **Map** p92 C4 ②④

Exotique can rightly claim to be the
best-stocked music store on the island
since the Virgin Megastore closed its
doors a few years ago; it also provides
DVD rentals of the latest Hollywood
releases and sells a range of high-tech
audio and visual equipment.
Other locations Bay Street Complex,
St George's Bay, St Julian's (2372
1600); Energy Complex, Republic
Street, Valletta (2124 1349); Malta
International Airport, Gudja (2167
3163); Arkadia Commercial Centre,
Victoria, Gozo (2155 8333).

Jeannine

30 Tower Road (2132 2297). **Open**
9.30am-1pm, 4.30-7pm Mon-Sat.
Map p93 D4 ②⑤

A shop packed with bags for every
occasion – be they sturdy leather bags
for work or delicate clutches to match
elegant evening dresses – and with a
strong focus on quality across the
entire range. Jeannine also stocks a
selection of shoes, sandals and belts.

Junction 66

66 Tower Road (2133 4451). **Open**
9am-1.15pm, 4-7.30pm Mon-Sat.
Map p93 D4 ②⑥

The colourful shop window of Junction
66 gives a good idea of the selection of
top-name designer domestic wares
waiting inside. The store stocks a vast
choice of fine glassware, silver cutlery
sets, dinner sets, bone china figurines,
vases, wooden clocks and much more,
with a range of styles catering to all
tastes from rustic and classic to more
artfully contemporary.
Other location Arkadia Commercial
Centre, Victoria, Gozo (2155 8333).

Max Mara

46-48 Tower Road (2134 1961).
Open 9.30am-1pm, 4-7pm Mon-Sat.
Map p93 D3 ②⑦

This Italian fashion label has established an international reputation for
promoting ultra-feminine styles
through its products. If you are looking for a classic item with a contemporary edge and an accent on quality –
and you're willing to spend a little more
than at more conventional big-brand
design branches – then this could well
be the store for you.

outlet caters its stock mainly to women, although there is a small selection of shirts, scarves and ties for men.

Next

Bisazza Street (2134 4156/www.next. co.uk). **Open** 9am-7pm Mon, Wed-Sat; 9am-1pm, 4-7pm Tue. **Map** p93 D4 ③⓪
One of the UK's largest clothing retailers also has a pretty solid fan base here in Malta. Outlets on the island aren't as big as those abroad, nor is the stock as extensive, but there is still a good selection of the latest clothing, shoes and accessories for men, women and children, most of it leaning towards the more conservative and classic end of the spectrum.
Other location 54 Zachary Street, Valletta (2125 1562).

Optika

17 The Strand (2133 5463). **Open** 9am-1pm, 4-7pm Mon-Sat. **Map** p93 D4 ③①
A well-established shop offering a wide selection of prescription glasses and sunglasses catering to all budgets and style agendas. The choice is seemingly endless, with a good range of specs from big name designers like Calvin Klein, Versace, Prada and many more. Service is efficient and the staff both friendly and helpful.

Plaza Shopping Centre

Bisazza Street (2134 3832/www.plaza-shopping.com). **Open** 9am-1pm, 4-7pm Mon-Sat. **Map** p93 D4 ③②
A perfect retail refuge from the scorching heat or pouring rain of the outside world, the Plaza houses a number of notable outlets over four floors, with Miss Selfridge and United Colors of Benetton snuggling up to Body Shop, Panama Jack and Toni & Guy. The centre also houses a McDonald's and a café on the third floor.

Square Deal

1 Manuel Dimech Street (2133 0072). **Open** 9.30am-7.30pm Mon-Fri; 9am-8pm Sat. **Map** p92 C4 ③③
A large outlet providing two floors of smart and casual clothes for both men and women, with a selection spanning

Mil Ideas

27 Tower Road (2133 3508). **Open** 9.30am-1.30pm, 4.30-7.30pm Mon-Sat. **Map** p93 D4 ②⑧
A vast range of decorative items for the home, from quirky candlesticks, vases and lampshades to straw placemats, frames and some seriously desirable imported jewellery. The shop is also well stocked with cards, wrapping paper, potpourri and incense, and prices tend to be very reasonable.
Other locations Republic Street, Valletta (2124 8385); Mil Ideas Showroom, Marina Street, Pietà (2124 8272).

Nara Camicie

1 Bisazza Street (2133 2587/www. naracamicie.com). **Open** 9.30am-7.30pm Mon-Sat. **Map** p93 D4 ②⑨
Nara Camicie makes beautiful shirts with a fantastic fit, using fine fabrics in a range of dazzling colours. The price tag is perfectly reasonable given the quality on offer, with shirts selling for an average €55.90, and while the selection isn't large, it does encompass everything from plain dress shirts to more elaborately frilled, beaded and otherwise embellished creations. The

a number of well-known brands along the lines of Celio, Calvin Klein, Tom Tailor and Tally Weijl, most of it at very reasonable prices.
Other location Energy Complex, Republic Street, Valletta (2123 4524).

Swarovski

NEW *69 Tower Road (2133 7447/www. swarovski.com).* **Open** 10am-7.30pm Mon-Sat. **Map** p93 D4 ③④
Everything sparkles at this recently opened outlet in the heart of Sliema, home to a large selection of Swarovski diamante jewellery. For the younger female, the contemporary line is particularly eye-catching – big, bold rings and stunning pendants featuring the most meticulously crafted crystals. Other items include purses and bags studded with crystals, as well as dainty key chains and decorative items for more distinguished homes.

TeamSport

Cathedral Street (2132 2514). **Open** 9.30am-7.30pm Mon-Sat. **Map** p93 D4 ③⑤
This recently expanded branch of TeamSport offers a wide selection of sportswear and shoes for men, women and children, and stocks internationally renowned brands such as Nike, Adidas, Reebok, Puma, Arena and Speedo. Staff are helpful and prices extremely reasonable.
Other location Gallarija Darmanin, Dun Karm Psaila Street, Iklin (2141 8891).

Ultimate

Bisazza Street (2131 8941/www. ultimate.com.mt). **Open** 9.30am-1.30pm, 4-7pm Mon-Fri; 9.30am-8pm Sat. **Map** p93 D4 ③⑥
A small store that's packed with a vast selection of hi-fi equipment, television sets, cameras, camcorders, phones and computer accessories, plus DVD players, mp3 players, iPods and assorted gadgets for modern living. The majority of stock is from big name brands.
Other locations Salvu Busuttil Street, San Gwann (2137 2663); 288 Victory Street, Qormi (2149 4804); Fleur De Lys Street, Birkirkara (2144 8644).

Urban Jungle

Bisazza Street (2131 2096). **Open** 9.30am-1.30pm, 4-7pm Mon-Fri; 9.30am-2pm, 3-7pm Sat. **Map** p93 D4 ③⑦
A chain stocking Nike sportswear for men, women and children alongside a wide selection of training shoes and sporting equipment for various disciplines – from basic health and fitness gear to outlandish accessories for more specialised pursuits.
Other locations Arkadia Commercial Centre, Gozo (2210 3000); 36 Republic Street, Valletta (2122 5623); Park Towers Mall, St Julian's (2137 8620).

VIP

Bisazza Street (2134 2466). **Open** 9am-1pm, 4-7pm Mon-Fri; 9.30am-1.30pm, 4-7pm Sat. **Map** p93 D4 ③⑧
VIP is a good place to start if you're looking for a formal executive gift, with a wide variety of exclusive office stationery, Swiss watches and leather briefcases. There are also accessories from international brands along the lines of Cartier, Piaget, Tag Heuer and Christian Dior, as well as less expensive labels such as Esprit and Swatch.
Other location Republic Street, Valletta (2122 4270).

Wallis

NEW *Tower Road (2131 6895).* **Open** 9.30am-7.30pm Mon-Sat. **Map** p93 D4 ③⑨
The international high street fashion store recently opened its doors in Malta and displays well-priced, high-quality items for the elegant modern woman. Clothes are somewhat conservative but the cuts are always original, smart and eminently attractive.

Zara

1 Tower Road (2132 3585/www.zara. com). **Open** 9.30am-7.30pm Mon-Sat. **Map** p93 D4 ④⓪
The Maltese branch of the popular Spanish fashion chain is housed on the premises of the former Alhambra cinema. The women's section, located on the ground floor, has quality wardrobe staples including suits, eveningwear, lingerie, shoes and bags, while the first has men's and a children's clothing.

MALTA BY AREA

Mdina

Mdina & Rabat

Perched atop a high plateau, Malta's former capital of Mdina is a veritable open-air museum rich with over 3,000 years of artistic heritage. The legacy of its original Roman occupants can be found inscribed in the mosaic paving of the **Domus Romana**, among the world's best-preserved Roman townhouses and a testament to Mdina's central role at the time.

Little is known and even less architectural evidence remains of the Arabs that occupied (and named) Mdina following the fall of the Romans, but the subsequent Christian era is well documented, with various chronicles recounting the siege of the city by Count Roger the Norman in 1091. The following centuries saw the establishment of a Christian community in Mdina and the consecration of various places of worship, with the Knights of St John in 1693 employing the Maltese architect Lorenzo Gafa to impose an ornate Baroque upgrade on central **St Paul's Cathedral** after the original building was damaged by an earthquake.

Other rich Baroque buildings in Mdina include the Magisterial Palace with its superb courtyard, today home to the **Museum of Natural History**; the newly restored **Palazzo Falson**; the Episcopal Seminary housing the **Cathedral Museum**; the Banca Giuratale or Municipal Palace (Triq Villegaignon); and Xara Palace (Council Square), the latter's 18th-century façade now home to a smart hotel. Take your time to wander, stopping for a break in Bastion Square, a small clearing behind Mdina's northwest ramparts.

Outside the fortified walls of the city is the town of Rabat, home to a fascinating complex of catacombs that suggest the existence of a once thriving Christian community living under repressive Roman rule: **St Agatha's** and **St Paul's Catacombs** are both well worth a visit. **St Paul's Grotto** is another subterranean wonder, reputedly the site from which St Paul preached in AD 60 after being shipwrecked on the island while travelling to Rome to stand trial, and drawing many centuries of pilgrims as a result.

A few kilometres south of Rabat is public Buskett Gardens, lush with natural springs and citrus groves, oaks, Aleppo pines and olive trees. Overlooking the garden is Verdala Palace (closed to the public), built by Grand Master de Verdalle as a country retreat and now serving a similar function for the president of Malta. Less than two kilometres south of Buskett Gardens is Malta's highest point, Dingli Cliffs, commanding views of the open ocean and a great spot to watch the sun set.

Sights & museums

Cathedral Museum

Archbishop Square, Mdina (2145 4697). **Open** 9am-4.30pm Mon-Fri; 9am-3.30pm Sat. **Admission** *Cathedral & Museum* free-€2.33. **Map** p107 C2 ❶

Set in an 18th-century Baroque build-ing formerly serving as a seminary, this fascinating museum displays countless religious artefacts and art-works acquired by nearby St Paul's Cathedral over the ages, including a series of copperplates and woodcuts by Albrecht Dürer, the latter especially outstanding for their detail and emo-tional resonance. Also on display are original indictments of the Inquisition, genealogical tables of the Knights, Roman pottery and a rare coin collec-tion dating back to the Carthaginians.

MALTA BY AREA

Rabat

0   200 m
0   200 yds
© Copyright Time Out Group 2008

TRIQ GHEREIXEM

TRIQ SAN

TRIQ P. MUSCAL

TRIQ BIR IR-RIEBU

TRIQ P. MUSCAL

Tad Dejr

St Agatha's Catacombs

TRIQ HAL

TRIQ QASIME

❶ Sights & museums
❶ Eating & drinking
❶ Shopping
❶ Nightlife
❶ Arts & leisure

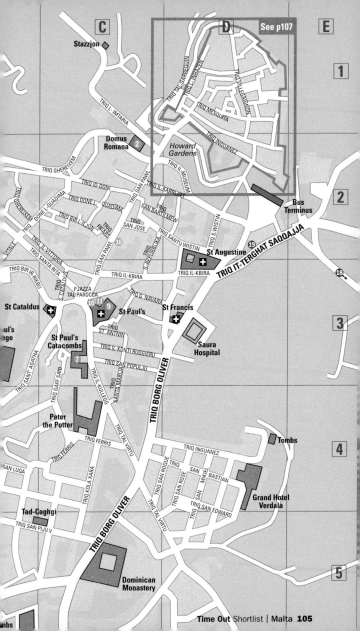

Stazzjon

TRIQ TAL-GARREWIIN

TRIQ L-IMTARIA

Domus Romana 2

Howard Gardens

TRIQ MESQUITA

TRIQ L-INHAXEN

TRIQ L-ERATON

TRIQ INGUANEZ

TRIQ GHEREXEM

TRIQ ID-DONI

TRIQ SAN PAWL

TRIQ IL-KARRUIR

TRIQ IL-MUSEUM

2

TRIQ DONE L-QUADMA

TRIQ ID-DONI L-QUADMA

TRIQ BIR L-ILJUN

TRIQ FRIARS

TRIQ SAN PAWL

TRIQ SAN BARTILMEW

TRIQ SAN JOSE

TRIQ SANTU WISTIN

TRIQ S. WISTIN

TRIQ SAN PAWL

St Augustine

Bus Terminus

TRIQ L-VITTORJA

TRIQ SANTA RITA

TRIQ IL-REPUBLIKA

16

TRIQ IR-REBU

TRIQ BIR

19

TRIQ IL-KBIRA

TRIQ IL-KBIRA

TRIQ IT-TERGHAT SAQQAJJA

18

St Cataldus

PJAZZA TAL-PAROCCA

TRIQ G. NAVARA

10 11

9

St Paul's

TRIQ ANTNIN

St Francis

3

TRIQ SANTA RITA

ul's ege

St Paul's Catacombs

7

TRIQ SANT'AGATHA

TRIQ IL-KONTI RUGGIERU

TRIQ SAN POPULJU

Saura Hospital

TRIQ GAFF SAID

TRIQ IL-KULLEGG

TRIQ SANTA MARIJA

TRIQ BORG OLIVER

Peter the Potter

TRIQ FERRIS

TRIQ TAL-VIRTU

Tombs

TRIQ INGUANEZ

4

TRIQ KOLA XARA

TRIQ FERRIS

TRIQ SAN ROQUE

TRIQ SAN ROSE

TRIQ SAN MIKIEL

TRIQ BASTIAN

SAN LUQA

Tad-Caghgi

TRIQ SAN PIJU V

TRIQ TAL-VIRTU

TRIQ SAN EDWARD

Grand Hotel Verdala

TRIQ BORG OLIVER

Dominican Monastery

5

mbs

Domus Romana

Museum Esplanade, Rabat (2145 4125/www.heritagemalta.org). **Open** 9am-5pm daily. **Admission** €5.82; €1.74-€2.91 reductions. **Map** p105 C2 ❷

The Domus Romana displays remains found on the site of the largest Roman house excavated in Malta, built around AD 50 and still boasting fine mosaic floors. Among the priceless exhibits on show are marble statues of famous Roman personalities and domestic items including amphorae, looms and glassware, as well as various finds of funerary and agricultural significance.

Mdina Dungeons

St Publius Square, Mdina (2145 0267). **Open** 10am-4.30pm daily. **Admission** €3.73; €1.86 reductions. **Map** p107 B3 ❸

Located in the former prisons of the Magisterial Palace built by the Knights upon entering Mdina, the local dungeons have been recreated as a rather grisly museum of Maltese torture throughout the ages, with life-size effigies depicting harrowing historical events such as the highly unpleasant martyrdom of St Agatha, the hacking of limbs from rebellious slaves and the slow deaths of prisoners withering in metal cages suspended in the courtyard. Younger children will either scream with delight or dismay.

Museum of Natural History

Vilhena Palace, St Publius Square, Mdina (2145 5951/www.heritage malta.org). **Open** 9am-5pm daily. **Admission** €2.33; €0.58-€1.16 reductions. **Map** p107 C3 ❹

The Museum of Natural History is housed in the Baroque Magisterial Palace, built by Grand Master Vilhena in 1724 and converted into a hospital during British rule. It holds exhibits on Malta's geological formation – a collection of over 10,000 rocks and minerals that's dry in more than one sense – alongside an abundance of local flora and fauna, exotic shells and insects. There is also a reference library on natural science for enthusiasts.

Palazzo Falson

Villegaignon Street, Mdina (2145 4512/www.palazzofalson.com). **Open** *July-Sept* 10am-5pm Tue-Fri (last visit 4pm); 10am-8pm Sat, Sun (last visit 7pm). *Oct-June* 10am-5pm Tue-Sun (last visit 4pm). **Admission** €10; free-€5 reductions. Under-5s not admitted. **Map** p107 B1 ❺

The recently restored Palazzo Falson is one of the oldest medieval buildings still standing in Mdina, with parts of the structure dating to the early 13th century. This historic house museum now houses a treasure trove of exhibits such as exotic armaments, antique jewellery, Roman amphorae, intricate oriental rugs and several priceless works of art including etchings by Albrecht Dürer and Mattia Preti's *Lucretia Stabbing Herself*. Other rooms including the bedroom, study and simple chapel are recreated with period furniture, offering a unique insight into the life of the historic Maltese nobility.

St Agatha's Catacombs

St Agatha Street, Rabat (2145 4503). **Open** *mid June-Sept* 9am-4.30pm Mon-Sat. *Oct-mid June* 9am-noon Mon-Fri; 9am-12.30pm Sat. *Tours* every 30mins. **Admission** €1.74. **Map** p104 B3 ❻

This subterranean maze is more spread out than nearby St Paul's Catacombs, but only the oldest part of the complex is open to the public, a fascinating series of chambers dug deep beneath a primitive rock-cut chapel. Near the entrance is a crypt with a carved altar and intriguing Byzantine frescoes depicting the Madonna, St Paul and St Agatha herself, who is reputed to have hidden down here for a period in AD 249 while fleeing Roman persecution in Catania.

St Paul's Catacombs

St Agatha Street, Rabat (2145 4562/www.heritagemalta.org). **Open** 9am-5pm daily. **Admission** €4.66; €1.16-€2.33 reductions. **Map** p105 C3 ❼

Early Christians were interred in St Paul's Catacombs while burials inside the city were prohibited under Roman law – a practice that continued as late

MALTA BY AREA

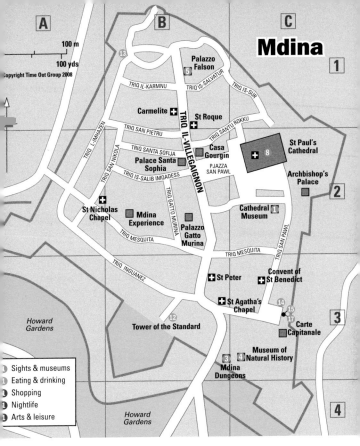

Mdina

100 m
100 yds

Copyright Time Out Group 2008

13

TRIQ IL-KARMNU

Palazzo
Falson

5

TRIQ IS-SALVATUR

TRIQ IS-SUR

Carmelite

St Roque

TRIQ SANTU ROKKU

TRIQ SAN PIETRU

TRIQ IL-VILLEGAIGNON

St Paul's
Cathedral

TRIQ L-IMHAZEN

TRIQ SANTA SOFIJA

Casa
Gourgin

8

TRIQ SAN NIKOLA

Palace Santa
Sophia

PJAZZA
SAN PAWL

Archbishop's
Palace

TRIQ IS-SALIB IMQADDES

2

St Nicholas
Chapel

TRIQ GATTO MURINA

Mdina
Experience

Cathedral
Museum

1

TRIQ SAN PAWL

Palazzo
Gatto Murina

TRIQ MESQUITA

TRIQ INGUANEZ

St Peter

Convent of
St Benedict

St Agatha's
Chapel

14

Howard
Gardens

12

Tower of the Standard

15
17

Carte
Capitanale

3

Sights & museums
Eating & drinking
Shopping
Nightlife
Arts & leisure

Museum of
Natural History

3

4

Mdina
Dungeons

Howard
Gardens

4

as the fourth century. These sprawling, interconnected caverns constitute an impressive honeycomb of tombs, with a primitive chapel at the entrance and passageways branching out in a haphazard manner – the only way to explore is to wander about and double back at the end of every blind alley.

St Paul's Cathedral

St Paul's Square, Mdina (no phone).
Open 9.30-11.45am Mon-Sat; 3-4.45pm
Sun. **Admission** *Cathedral & Museum*
€2.33. **Map** p107 C2 ⑧

The current building was designed in the late 17th century by Lorenzo Gafa, Malta's most famous architect, after the original Norman church was destroyed in an earthquake. Today's St Paul's is a grand religious monument in the heart of the city, beautifully proportioned and with a fine dome and elegant bell towers. The interior offers a patchwork of marble tombstones commemorating clergy and nobility, with large ceiling frescoes depicting St Paul preaching to the masses, while the chapels on either side of the chancel have ceiling frescoes and intricate floors of inlaid marble. Behind the main altar is a large painting of St Paul's conversion by Mattia Preti.

St Paul's Church

St Paul's Square, Rabat (no phone). **Open** 9am-5pm Mon-Sat. **Admission** free. **Map** p105 C3 **9**

Rebuilt in the Baroque style in 1653, the curvaceous exterior of St Paul's Church has an unusual design, with a complete lack of bell towers and a dome set well back from the façade. The interior is also strangely simple, but there are paintings at the back of the chancel that depict St Paul's shipwreck, St Publius and the Eucharist.

St Paul's Grotto

St Paul's Square, Rabat (no phone). **Open** 9am-5pm daily. **Admission** free. **Map** p105 C3 **10**

Following his shipwreck in Malta in AD 60, St Paul is alleged to have slept in this small underground cave during his three-month stay on the island, a time he spent preaching and baptising the Maltese community at large. The grotto has few embellishments or noteworthy objects save for a statue of the saint, a silver model of a Maltese galley donated by the Knights and lamps given by Pope Paul VI.

Wignacourt Museum

St Paul's Square, Rabat (2145 1060). **Open** 10am-3pm Mon-Sat. **Admission** €2.33. **Map** p105 C3 **11**

This former hostel for pilgrims visiting St Paul's Grotto is now a museum displaying religious artefacts amassed by the local parish over the ages – a somewhat disparate collection of wooden sculptures, vestments and works of art including a sombre series of paintings by Francesco Zhara.

Eating & drinking

Bacchus

1 Inguanez Street, Mdina (2145 4981/www.bacchus.com.mt). **Open** noon-11pm daily. **€€€**. **French**. **Map** p107 B3 **12**

Pricey and eminently popular, highlights on Bacchus's forward-thinking menu include courgettes stuffed with crab, French onion soup, and pork rolled in prosciutto. Seating comes either in a vaulted interior with stone floors or a more romantic terrace.

Ciappetti

5 St Agatha's Esplanade, Mdina (2145 9987). **Open** 11.30am-3pm, 7-10pm Tue-Sat; 11.30am-3pm Sun. **€€**. **Mediterranean**. **Map** p107 B1 **13**

Ciappetti is an oasis of calm whether you choose to dine indoors, within the typically Maltese courtyard or on the breathtaking terrace. Once you've soaked up the beauty, tuck into a starting platter of olives, sun-dried tomatoes and Maltese cheeses, or plump for one of the hearty mains – lamb shanks, fillet beef and tender chicken livers.

Fontanella Tea Gardens

1 Bastion Square, Mdina (2145 0208). **Open** *June-Sept* 10am-10.45pm daily. *Oct-May* 10am-6pm daily. **Café**. **Map** p107 C3 **14**

The cakes at this popular café are so good that certain local restaurants stock up and pass them off as their own, but avoid the pies and pizzas, which are less special. If possible, bag a table on the lofty terrace.

De Mondion Restaurant

Xara Palace Relais & Chateaux, Council Square, Mdina (2145 0560). **Open** 7.30-10.30pm Mon-Sat. **€€€€**. **French**. **Map** p107 C3 **15**

High on any food connoisseur's list of Malta's best restaurants, reassuringly expensive De Mondion – housed in a charming hotel – oozes style and elegance. So too with the outstanding seasonal menu, which features the likes of lamb fillets in madeira and nutmeg, and rabbit with creamy vanilla risotto.

Ristorante Cosmana Navarra

28 St Paul's Street, Rabat (2145 0638). **Open** 12.30-3.30pm Mon; 12.30-3.30pm, 6.30-10.30pm Tue-Sun. **€€**. **Mediterranean**. **Map** p105 C2 **16**

Cosmana, born in the 17th century, was the foundress of nearby St Paul's Church and once resided in the townhouse now home to this charming restaurant. Fridays bring *fenkata* nights with signature pan-fried rabbit in garlic and wine, while other dishes include beef bourguignon and sautéed chicken with porcini mushrooms.

Trattoria AD 1530

Xara Palace Relais & Chateaux, Council Square, Mdina (2145 0560). **Open** 10.30am-2.30pm, 6-10.30pm Mon-Thur; 11.30am-11pm Fri-Sun. Closed Tue Nov-Apr. **€€**. **Mediterranean**. **Map** p107 C3 ⑰

An informal eaterie in the Xara Palace Relais & Chateaux hotel offering traditional Mediterranean dishes including salmon ravioli, cannelloni with spinach and ricotta and meat or fish dishes such as quail in honey and lemon.

Nightlife

Gianpula/Molecule

Rabat (2145 0238/www.gianpula.com). **Open** *June-Sept* 10pm-4am Fri; 11pm-4am Sat. **Admission** €5.82-€15.14. **Map** p105 E3 ⑱

Parties at this open-air club come courtesy of Malta's biggest promoters as well as international names like Pacha, Ministry of Sound and Godskitchen. Located in an old farmhouse with sprawling grounds, this Ibiza-style club features a swimming pool and seven bars and has hosted DJs such as Tiesto, Sasha and Erick Morillo. Molecule is Gianpula's VIP club, used exclusively during the winter months.

Tattingers Club

Saqqajja Hill, Rabat (2145 1104/www. tattingers.com). **Open** 9pm-4am Fri-Sun. **Admission** €4. **Map** p105 D2 ⑲

Tattingers is an indoor club playing techno, progressive house and trance to an in-the-know crowd, many of them locals. Its isolated location lends the air of a semi-legal rave, although it's a well-designed venue pulling in big name DJs from the Balearic circuit and international promoters.

A sweet for all seasons

Year-round excuses to indulge in dessert.

Lent: Kwarezimal

These charming almond and honey biscuits are traditionally eaten during Lent due to the fact that they were historically one of few things fasting Catholics were permitted to consume during that period (the name comes from the Maltese for '40 days').

Easter: Figolla

Large cakes made of sweet vanilla dough, filled with almond paste and topped with colourful icing. The first figolla of Easter morning is by custom the first luxury item eaten following the 40-day fast, and the cakes are traditionally shaped into images of religious significance such as lambs, fishes or hearts.

Winter: Pudina ta' l-Hobz

This warming bread pudding becomes increasingly popular as the chill winter evenings draw in. Like the English equivalent, it's an excellent way of using up stale bread, and is flavoured with milk, cocoa, dried fruits and a splash of liqueur.

Christmas: Qaghaq ta' l-Ghasel

These light pastry rings are slashed with a knife before baking so that they come out of the oven literally bursting with a thick, dark centre of treacle and jam. A Christmas delicacy that you'll also find served with coffee all year round.

MALTA BY AREA

Bugibba

The Rest of Malta

Bugibba, Mellieha & Around

Bugibba emerged as Malta's prime resort town with the advent of mass tourism in the 1960s, and the peninsula on which it stands, flanked by two large bays, has become a tight mass of multistorey apartment blocks and hotels. Most of the action takes place in the aptly named Tourists Street and pedestrianised Bay Square, both teeming with bars and cafés, but the town's more authentic character is evident at its southwestern extremity, home to **St Paul's Shipwreck Church** and a small cove filled with colourful boats.

This is the spot where Bugibba merges with St Paul's Bay, an erstwhile fishermen's hamlet today dominated by an anonymous fringe of modern hotels and apartment blocks. It is more tranquil and less hectic than Bugibba, with a sweet scattering of boats anchored in the bay and an old town centre – based around the parish church – filled with pretty old houses, and with the historic **Wignacourt Tower** a short walk due west.

Beyond St Paul's Bay the road snakes up a steep slope towards Mellieha, the attractive town centre of which has long been a place of pilgrimage for those flocking to its subterranean rock-cut chapel, the Grotto of Our Lady (Gorg Borg Olivier Street) – bare of adornments save a reputedly miraculous statue of the Madonna – or to the shrine in the nearby **Church of Our Lady of Mellieha**, its walls covered with votive offerings left by those healed through divine benevolence. Across the valley is the mysterious Gharukaza – which is a literal embodiment of its name (*ghar* means 'cave', while *casa* is Italian for house), and still reputedly home to an old man who lives in the most basic conditions without electricity or running water.

Within the limits of Mellieha is the island's single largest sandy beach, Mellieha Bay (also known as Ghadira Bay, see box p114), home to the **Adira Sailing Centre & Lido**, which hires out kite surfers (from October to mid May), windsurfers and sailing dinghies (all year round). West of the bay, the land rises again to a rugged plateau dominated by the Red Tower (open 10am-1pm Mon-Sat, admission €1.16), one of the most attractive fortifications erected by the Knights; the view from its roof is among Malta's finest, taking in the scenic spread of Mellieha Bay on one side and stretching all the way to Gozo and Comino on the other. Further west, the rugged terrain gives way to sandy beaches scooped out of the shore at the northwestern extremity of Malta, including Paradise Bay (see box p114), girdled by dramatic cliffs.

Sights & museums

Church of Our Lady of Mellieha

Mellieha (no phone). **Open** 8am-noon, 5-7pm daily. **Admission** free.
Originally serving as a small crypt in the medieval age, this church has been extended and expanded several times over the centuries to accommodate the swelling numbers of pilgrims making their way to its reputedly healing shrine. The current building – which houses a fantastic mosaic of the Madonna – dates from the 17th century, and the walls of its corridors are covered with votive offerings in thanksgiving for miraculous healings.

Mellieha

St Paul's Shipwreck Church

Church Street, Bugibba (no phone). **Open** 6.30-8am, 6-8pm daily. **Admission** free.
Tradition holds that the galley on which St Paul was travelling to stand trial in Rome was wrecked on the rocks around Malta during a storm, with the saint reputed to have scrambled ashore at exactly the spot where this small chapel stands. The current building was built in 1958 after a World War II bomb destroyed the original church.

Wignacourt Tower

St Gerard Street, St Paul's Bay (2121 5222). **Open** 9.30am-noon Mon, Thur-Sun; 9.30am-noon, 1-3pm Wed. **Admission** €1.16.
Erected by the Knights in the early 17th century to guard St Paul's Bay, fortified Wignacourt Tower today holds an interesting permanent exhibition exploring the form and function of the Knights' military architecture across the islands, as well as a small selection of arms and armour.

MALTA BY AREA

Naxxar p118

Eating & drinking

Adira Sailing Centre & Lido

Marfa Road, Mellieha Bay, Mellieha (2152 3190). **Open** 11am-10pm daily. €€. **Mediterranean**.

Malta's first sailing centre serves incredibly fresh fish dishes on a shaded terrace overlooking Mellieha Bay, while those who'd rather eat while basking on the beach itself will be pleased to find that the ground-floor bar serves snacks, sandwiches and healthy salads throughout the day. Those looking to burn off the calories can rent seagoing vessels on site.

The Arches

113 Main Street, Mellieha (2152 3460/www.thearchesmalta.com). **Open** 7-10.30pm Mon-Sat. €€€€. **French**.

The Arches is something of a Maltese culinary institution thanks to a combination of excellent service, an impressive wine list and outstanding French cuisine served in an elegant formal setting. This is fine dining at its best, from starters like cold poached lobster or creamy French onion soup to mains along the lines of whole sea bass, lobster thermidor, grilled grouper fish and a variety of sublime meat dishes.

Essence

Radisson SAS Golden Sands Resort & Spa, Golden Bay, Mellieha (2356 1000/www.goldensands.com.mt). **Open** 7.30-10pm Tue-Sat. €€€€. **French**.

By far and away one of the most exciting restaurants in Malta, Essence is fancy without being fussy, smart without being stuffy and boasts an innovative menu featuring dishes such as liquorice-infused John Dory with cauliflower purée and a masterful veal trio comprised of slow-cooked fillet, pan-fried sweetbreads and braised shoulder with root vegetables.

Giuseppi's Wine Bar & Restaurant

Main Street, Mellieha (2157 4882). **Open** 7.30-10.30pm Tue-Sat. €€. **Mediterranean**.

Out-of-town regulars drive a long way (by Maltese standards) to savour the outstanding yet reasonably priced dishes prepared by chef-patron Michael Diacono at this landmark restaurant. Food is served in a charming townhouse on two floors adorned with antique furnishings that only add to the authentic, oddly timeless feel of the place. The menu changes regularly but always includes dishes displaying an innovative spirit and an eye for the fantastic, from rabbit richly infused with chocolate sauce to tuna toasted with coffee, as well as more conventional dishes like king prawns or tender lamb served with couscous and rocket. Giuseppi's is well worth a visit, but be sure to book long in advance.

Il Padrino

San Remo Beach Club, Mellieha Bay, Mellieha (2157 3326). **Open** 6-10.30pm daily. €€. **Mediterranean**.

One of the real pleasures of a Maltese summer is eating fresh food on a sandy beach, and Il Padrino offers exactly that. The best time to go is around 7pm, when the scorching heat turns to a balmy evening warmth and the sun begins to set spectacularly. Highlights on the menu include the Il Padrino special beef fillet with a lovely seafood sauce and a range of lighter options including pizzas and salads, while the upmarket San Remo Beach Club below is a beach bum's paradise, renting sunbeds and with an affiliated watersports centre offering paragliding, sausage and ringo rides, as well as canoes and paddle boats for hire.

Palazzo Santa Rosa

Mistra Bay (2158 2737). **Open** 12.30-10.30pm Tue-Sun. €€€. **Mediterranean**.

It involves a fair old drive, a considerable amount of cash and a bit of a wait for the food to turn up, but once it does you're sure to forget your efforts. Chef-patron Claude Camilleri is a believer in good things taking time, and this restaurant has become something of a legend in Malta due to its refusal to

MALTA BY AREA

Going with the grains

Malta has beautiful sandy beaches aplenty
– you just have to know where to look.

Its southern Mediterranean location and reputation for watersports notwithstanding, Malta doesn't have quite so many sandy beaches as you might imagine. Head north, however, and you'll be well rewarded at **Mellieha Bay** (also known as Ghadira Bay) in Mellieha, the largest expanse of sand on the whole of the Maltese coast. It does get rather crowded in the high season (from June to September), but it's a great place to swim and as popular with adrenalin-fuelled watersports enthusiasts as it is with those less energetic punters sunning themselves on the terraces of its numerous beachside bars.

An altogether more relaxing atmosphere reigns at the slightly more southerly **Selmun Bay** (also known as Mgiebah Bay), which avoids the crowds thanks to its remote location (you'll have to follow a long, narrow lane and then scramble down a steep hill to get to the beach itself) and complete absence of amenities: bring a picnic, as there are no cafés or kiosks. **Paradise Bay** at Cirkewwa, on the northerly Marfa Peninsula, is also fairly secluded, enjoying a gorgeous setting on a natural cove but boasting some very good eating and drinking facilities and close proximity to the Paradise Bay Resort Hotel (2152 1166, www.paradise-bay.com), which also operates an excellent dive school.

The most popular beach on the west coast is **Golden Bay** (misleadingly named – the sand is actually more grey-brown), while neighbouring **Ghajn Tuffieha Bay**, accessed by a flight of 186 steps from the car park, offers a smaller, more secluded and infinitely more attractive alternative. There's also sand in the south at **Pretty Bay** in Birzebbuga, its seafront lined with a bustling mix of restaurants, cafés and colourful bars.

Over in Gozo, try the sublime red sands of northwesterly **Ramla Bay** – also teeming with tourists in the summer months, although it's delightfully quiet out of season – or neighbouring **San Blas Bay**, rockier but typically quieter and with clear, shallow waters perfect for snorkelling adventures.

rush anything. Set on an enormous estate commanding beautiful bay views – lovely as the sun sets – Palazzo Santa Rosa offers the likes of freshly made tagliatelle with sea urchins topped with caviar, fresh spaghetti with botargo (cured fish roe), an outstanding Bistecca Fiorentina, seared tuna and rare Maltese veal, and the extensive wine list is as carefully thought out as the cooking itself.

Porto Del Sol

13 Xemxija Hill, Xemxija (2157 3970). **Open** noon-2.30pm, 6-10.30pm Mon-Sat; noon-2.30pm Sun. Closed Sun June-Sept. €€. **Mediterranean**.

A vast menu of quality Mediterranean dishes is on offer at this comfortable restaurant with its window views of colourful boats and local fishermen going about their business. Not surprisingly, fish is the main draw, cooked simply and to the customer's preference, and the amiable owner Anthony is more than happy to recommend wines from an extensive list, or explain his specials, most of them based around the seasonal fish harvest.

Ristorante Savini

Qawra Road, Qawra (2157 6927). **Open** *mid Apr-Oct* 7-11pm daily. *Nov-mid Apr* 1pm Mon-Sat. €€. **Mediterranean**.

Avant-garde Mediterranean dishes are here served in an impeccably restored farmhouse with beautiful original features throughout. The frequently changing menu is creative, rich and generous of portion, with a regular favourite being the chef's own fillet of tender Irish beef in a light lobster sauce, and with a range of delicious own-made desserts to finish. Seating is always with a view; in the colder months, tables overlook the pretty courtyard and there's alfresco terrace dining in the summer months.

Rookie's Sports Bar & Grill

Sponges Street, Bugibba (2157 4550/www.rookiesmalta.com). **Open** 9pm-3am daily. **Bar**.

Just off Bugibba's main square, Rookie's is a haven for sports enthusiasts thanks to the regular sporting events beamed across its 14 separate televisions and two giant screens – football, rugby, racing, boxing, basketball and more, with up to nine events being shown at any given time. The bar also stages live music from some of Malta's best bands, plus there's good food and a friendly atmosphere drawing a mix of both locals and tourists back time and again.

Star of India

Xemxija Hill, Xemxija (2157 3682). **Open** *June-Sept* noon-3pm, 7-11pm daily. *Oct-May* noon-3pm Sun. €€. **Indian**.

With a location at the top of looming Xemxija hill, the Star offers spectacular views to accompany its top-notch Indian cuisine, which blends all manner of authentic ingredients to create a variety of delicious dishes, with a large proportion of fish curries alongside the usual meat-based mains and a range of traditional Indian sweets making for a dessert less ordinary.

Tal-Kaptan

Qawra Coast Road, Qawra (2157 7101/www.suncresthotel.com). **Open** *mid June-mid Sept* 9am-5pm, 6-10pm daily. *Mid Sept-mid June* 9am-5.30pm Mon-Thur, Sun; 9am-5.30pm, 6-9.30pm Fri, Sat. €€. **Mediterranean**.

Tal-Kaptan serves great views of Qawra Bay along with some of the best pizzas on the island in a nautical-themed restaurant that has gained a reputation for fresh ingredients and generous portions over 15 years of service. The Suncrest Special pizza is a firm favourite, mixing caponata (Sicilian aubergine relish) with Maltese sausage, while the Tal-Kaptan pizza is loaded with seafood.

Il-Veccja Restaurant & Wine Bar

372 St Paul's Street, St Paul's Bay (2158 2376). **Open** *June-Oct* 7-10.30pm daily. *Nov-May* 7-10.30pm Tue-Sun. €€. **Mediterranean**.

The Maltese fishing boat stranded at the entrance to Il-Veċċja gives some indication of the restaurant's affiliation with fresh fish, the majority of which is marinated in a simple wine and lemon mixture before being minimally cooked on a charcoal grill to retain the flavour. Traditional rabbit stewed with tomatoes also comes highly recommended. On summer evenings there's the opportunity to dine on a terrace perched over St Paul's Bay with fantastic ocean views, while an intimate wine bar underneath the main restaurant pulls in a younger crowd.

Wagon Steak House

Pioneer Road, Bugibba (2158 0666).
Open *July-Sept* 6.30-11.30pm daily.
Oct-June 6.30-11.30pm Mon-Sat;
noon-3.30pm, 6.30-11.30pm Sun.
€€€. North American.
Meat-lovers are more than welcome at this Wild West-themed steak house serving excellent cuts of mostly grilled meat, with more outlandish alternatives to conventional steaks including horsemeat, wild boar and venison. The decor is colourful and creative and a party atmosphere reigns supreme during the height of summer.

Nightlife

Amazonia Nightclub

The Promenade, Bugibba (2355 2355/www.amazoniamalta.com).
Open *mid June-Sept* 10pm-4am daily. *Oct-mid June* times vary.
Admission free Mon, Tue, Thur, Fri; varies Wed, Sat, Sun.
By day a beach complex and by night a clubber's paradise, Amazonia offers dancing by the water's edge and an exotic ambience bolstered by lagoon-style pools and palm trees. DJs spin everything from salsa and pop to uptempo house, while the crowd constitutes a mix of hip tourists, locals and students. If all that dancing gives you an appetite, the Batubulan terrace grill at the water's edge serves great salads during the day and barbecued meats in the evening. A place that ticks more than its fair share of clubbing boxes.

Beachaven

Xemxija Hill, Xemxija (2157 3682). **Open** 10pm-2am Fri, Sat. **Admission** free.
Located in a beach complex set aside from the main road and with sweeping ocean views as standard, Beachaven is rocking most weekends with locals and tourists letting their hair down to a carefree mix of pop, cheese and – later in the night – more upfront dance. During the day, punters can pay for a lounger and while away the afternoon sunning themselves to some superbly chilled tunes, while those visiting by boat will find on-site mooring facilities from June to September.

Arts & leisure

Empire Cinema

Pioneer Road, Bugibba (2158 1787).
Tickets €5.82; €3.49 reductions.
The only cinema in the northwest of Malta, the Empire shows Hollywood films and major releases across seven screens, and is a popular meeting place for Bugibba's younger crowd.

Mediterraneo Marine Park

Bahar ic-Caghaq (2137 2218/ www.mediterraneo.com.mt). **Open** *Apr-mid Oct* 10am-5pm. **Admission** €15.50; €10.50 reductions.
A popular sea and birdlife centre with animal shows aplenty (see box p119).

Oracle Casino

Dolmen Hotel, Dolmen Street, Qawra (2157 0057/www.oraclecasino.com).
Open *Slot machines* 10am-4am daily. *Gaming tables* noon-4am daily.
Admission free.
Would-be high rollers rejoice! This modern seafront casino is equipped with an abundance of slot machines and gaming tables running roulette, blackjack and stud poker, with two high-stakes tables for big spenders. The dress code is smart casual and ID will be required on a first visit: foreign nationals have to be over 18 to be allowed on the premises.
Other locations The Casino, Portomaso, St Julian's (2310 5555).

Mosta Dome p118

Popeye Village

Anchor Bay, Mellieha (2152 4782/ www.popeyemalta.com). **Open** *Jan, Feb* 9.30am-4.30pm daily. *Mar-May, Oct* 9.30am-5.30pm daily. *June-Sept* 9.30am-7pm daily. **Admission** €8; €6 reductions.

The *Popeye* film set (see box p119).

Splash & Fun Water Park

White Rocks, Coast Road, Bahar ic-Caghaq (2137 4283). **Open** *Apr-Oct* 9am-7pm daily. **Admission** €18; €10 reductions.

Slides and pools aplenty at the island's biggest water park (see box p119).

Mosta, Ta'Qali & the Three Villages

Northwest of Rabat is Mosta, home to the enormous church popularly known as the **Mosta Dome** – an appropriate moniker given that its enormous dome (claimed to be the third largest in Europe) is visible for miles around. Further south is Ta' Qali, home to the **Ta' Qali Crafts Village** and the **Malta Aviation Museum**, which provides an insight into World War II as it looked from the skies above Malta.

For a glimpse of quaint Maltese village life largely unchanged by the passing of time, while away a day wandering around Attard, Balzan and Lija (p42), known as the Three Villages because of their close proximity to each other and teeming with handsome baroque buildings set in quiet shaded alleys, plus an abundance of fine churches and chapels. Visit **San Anton Gardens**, originally part of the grounds adjoining the Grand Master's Palace, which these days serves as the official residence of the President of Malta. Nearby Naxxar is home to the sprawling **Palazzo Parisio & Gardens**, among Malta's most magnificently landscaped open spaces.

Sights & museums

Malta Aviation Museum

Ta' Qali (2141 6095/www.malta aviationmuseum.com). **Open** 9am-5pm daily. **Admission** €4.08; €1.16 reductions.

From 1938 to 1963 the area known as Ta' Qali served as Malta's first civil airport and the hub of its fighter aircraft in World War II, a heritage reflected in this expansive aviation museum. Among the collection are numerous aircraft including a Spitfire based at Ta' Qali during the war and a Hawker Hurricane recovered from the seabed off Wied iz-Zurrieq after spending some 54 years underwater. The museum also recently acquired a DC-3, an aircraft created in 1944 by the Douglas Aeroplane Company, which employed thousands of women – affectionately known as Rosie Riveters – who left their names and addresses hidden in the plane's various panels and shafts, thus leading to countless epistolary romances with Air Force mechanics who later stumbled upon them.

Mosta Dome

Rotunda Square, Mosta (2143 3826). **Open** 9-11.45am, 3-5pm daily. **Admission** free.

The dome of this formidable church is reputed to be Europe's third largest, while its cavernous interior boasts an elaborate geometric marble floor and – on the underside of the dome – an eye-catching pattern of blue Baroque flowers set against a glimmering gold background. Most of the countless pilgrims who come here, however, do so to pay homage to the Miracle of St Mary: during World War II, an enemy bomb pierced the dome and skittered across the floor among the congregation, which was attending Mass at the time, but failed to explode. A replica of the bomb is displayed in the sacristy.

Palazzo Parisio & Gardens

Victory Square, Naxxar (2141 2461/ www.palazzoparisio.com). **Open** 9am-4pm Mon-Fri. *Tours* on the hr. **Admission** €8.15; €4-€5.24 reductions.

A magnificent and privately owned palazzo originally built in 1733 by the Portuguese Grand Master Manoel de Vilhena. Many of its features – including the ornate mirrored ballroom – are the work of Maltese craftsmen, and the extensive gardens rank among the islands' finest. The grounds of the palazzo are also home to the charming Café Luna (see below).

San Anton Gardens

Triq Lord Strickland, Attard (2141 1111). **Open** varies. **Admission** free.
Formerly part of the adjoining Grand Master's Palace (now the official residence of the Maltese President and unsurprisingly closed to the public), San Anton Gardens provides a welcome sanctuary of tranquil ponds, fragrant flowerbeds and vividly colourful trees all teeming with birdlife (although the unkempt aviaries are best avoided). The perfect place to unwind with a book and a wonderful spot to break up an afternoon spent wandering around the Three Villages.

Eating & drinking

Café Luna

NEW *Palazzo Parisio, Victory Square, Naxxar (2141 2461).* **Open** 9am-6pm Mon-Sat. **Café**.
This café-restaurant has a fantastic location in the stunning 18th-century Palazzo Parisio, and boasts a pretty, pastel pink interior and, for summer dining, elegantly laid tables basking in the palazzo's beautiful gardens: with such a sumptuous backdrop, and with so many waiters flitting about the paths in formal cream uniforms, it becomes easy to imagine oneself at an upmarket garden party. The menu isn't particularly imaginative (think along the lines of more straightforward pasta dishes, salads and cakes), but the food is well presented and generally delicious, the staff attentive and there's a good selection of wines.

Etienne Locum Vinim

13 Triq Il-Kbira, Attard (2142 4647). **Open** varies. **€€€**. **Fusion**.

Just kidding

Pint-sized adventures on the northwestern coast.

Families will find several major attractions on the coast around Bugibba and Mellieha capable of putting smiles on kids' faces. Dolphins and sea lions are stars of the show at the wet and very wild **Mediterraneo Marine Park** (p116), which offers adults and children over eight the chance to swim with dolphins. For those who prefer feathered to fishy fun, there's also a parrot show.

From animal magic to good, old-fashioned splashing around, the neighbouring **Splash and Fun Water Park** (p118) is the perfect place for little ones to cool off in summer, with water slides ranging from sedate to scream-inducing, a wave pool breaking at up to 1.5 metres (five feet), plus various group activities including dancing, volleyball and aerobics. For smaller kids, the Children's Splash Land has fun features such as arching jets, water guns and a tunnel slide.

Finally, kids will be too young to remember the film (critical mauling of which almost ruined its director, Robert Altman), but **Popeye Village** (p118) is the actual set from the 1980 Robin Williams movie *Popeye* – an entire village of wooden houses, some converted into bars and shops, others equipped with props from shooting. Sections of the film are screened in a small cinema, plus there are swimming pools, glassblowing workshops, summer boat rides around the bay and, for exhausted adults, a Popeye-themed winery. Glass of Bluto Red, anyone?

A Maltese culinary institution, Etienne Locum Vinim splits its setting in an old stone building in the centre of Attard between a more basic downstairs restaurant serving pizza and pasta and an adventurous ground-floor space where the owner gets to exercise his inside knowledge of and affection for fine food, cooking up endlessly creative Mediterranean dishes, many of them with a unique Asian twist. The place is also an oenophile's heaven, with an extensive wine list and a special menu that pairs individual courses with vintages to enhance their various flavours.

Lord Nelson

278 Main Street, Mosta (2143 2590). **Open** 7.30-10.30pm Tue-Sat. Closed 1wk Jan & 2wks Aug. €€€. **Mediterranean**.
The Lord Nelson may be a short drive off the beaten track, but shouldn't be missed by those looking for some of the finest cooking Malta has to offer. Starters include the likes of pan-fried calf's liver and duck ravioli with wild mushrooms and cream, with mains along the lines of poached salmon with a fennel purée and boned rabbit legs with pancetta, and with a divine crème brulée heading up the list of sumptuous desserts. All that and a charming location in a 300-year-old townhouse with balcony views of the majestic Mosta Dome. Just don't risk making the journey without a reservation.

Ta' Marija

Constitution Street, Mosta (2143 4444/www.tamarija.com). **Open** 10am-3pm, 6-11.30pm Mon-Sat; 10am-3pm Sun. €€€. **Maltese**.
A family-run restaurant serving real Maltese food with an authentic sense of local hospitality, and with traditional island music and dancing on selected evenings. Homely dishes include the likes of ricotta ravioli in a tomato and basil sauce, stuffed aubergines and beef olives with Maltese sausage, while more adventurous concoctions – all inspired by Maltese recipes and ingredients – include a carrot, orange and ginger soup and quails marinated in Maltese honey. The wine list is also worth mentioning, with ten of its 12 pages dedicated to local wines.

Shopping

Ta' Qali Crafts Village

Ta Qali (www.taqali.com). **Open** times vary.
This collection of artisans' workshops is one of Malta's most unusual shopping experiences, not to mention one of the finest places to stock up on locally handcrafted gifts. The workshops – operating out of old Nissen huts on Ta Qali's former World War II airfield – cover everything from carpenters and furniture makers to jewellers, glassblowers, metalworkers and lace makers. Prices aren't always low but the quality is the unique setting is worth the journey alone.

Nightlife

Club Numero Uno

Ta' Qali Crafts Village, Ta' Qali (2135 8078/www.clubnumerouno.com). **Open** *June-Sept* 10.30pm-4am Sat, Sun. **Admission** €4.66-€6.99.
Open only in summer, outdoor club Numero Uno attracts a hip crowd and has an exotic, Asian feel thanks to the massive wicker canopy shrouding the dancefloor, which can hold up to 1,000 people. Music ranges from rock to R&B in the early hours, but expect house DJs to rule the night before long. There is also an elevated VIP area with waitress service – phone ahead to book a table.

Arts & leisure

National Stadium

Ta Qali (2143 6137). **Open** times vary. **Tickets** prices vary.
The Maltese nation is football mad, and the games that garner the most public hysteria – both national and international – take place at this enormous stadium, built in 1980 with a standing capacity of 17,000. The stadium is also home to a full-size swimming pool and an extensive gym.

MALTA BY AREA

Marsaxlokk

Southeast Malta

It's fair to say that there are fewer cultural draws in the southeastern reaches of the island, although history buffs will happily lap up the looming fortifications of St Thomas Tower in Marsascala, built by the Knights in 1614 and still stunning, if sadly closed to the public. Nor is a week in Malta complete without a trip to the Sunday fish market at Marsaxlokk, where local boats ply their wares before they're snapped up and shipped off to the island's best restaurants; be sure to get there early in the morning if you want to see the best stuff on display, as most of it tends to be bought up by lunchtime.

A drive south of Marsaxlokk, Birzebugga is home to the highly mysterious **Ghar Dalam Cave & Museum**, while the nearby Ghar Hasan Cave is believed to have once served as a hiding place for a notorious 12th-century Saracen rebel, and provides a truly eerie wander by torchlight. Nearby,

the Playmobil Funpark (Hal Far Industrial Estate, Birzebugga, 2224 2445, www.playmobilmalta.com) caters to small children with a large play area, a toyshop and various colourful character displays.

Zurrieq, further west, is the site of several charming windmills and the parish St Catherine's Church, home to an interesting altarpiece painted by Mattia Preti during a time when the artist was seeking sanctuary here during an outbreak of plague, while the 15th-century Chapel of the Annunciation, in the nearby settlement of Hal Millieri, houses some very interesting 15th-century frescoes (open 9.30am-noon first Sunday of the month). Slightly further south, boats depart from Wied iz-Zurrieq for the famous stone arch of the Blue Grotto, a 30-minute sail away.

Further west still is Qrendi, where the bizarre **Hagar Qim** and **Mnajdra Temples** offer fascinating windows into the astrological inclinations of the most ancient Maltese societies.

MALTA BY AREA

Ghar Dalam
Cave & Museum

Birzebugga (2295 4000). **Open**
9am-5pm daily. **Admission**
€3.49; €1.16 reductions.

This remarkable cave – the name of
which is aptly translated as 'Cave of
Darkness' – stretches 144m (472ft) into
the limestone bedrock of Birzebugga,
and it was here that the earliest evidence of settlement on the island was
discovered, with human remains dating back some 7,400 years. The lower
levels, which date back up to 500,000
years, contain the fossilised remains of
animals such as dwarf elephants and
hippopotamuses, which roamed Malta
when it was still joined to Italy. The
first 50m (164ft) are open to the public,
while an on-site museum showcases
the most interesting finds, including
assembled skeletons and fossilised
teeth preserved in Victorian-style spec-
imen jars. Certain to bring out the intrepid explorer in children.

Hagar Qim

*Qrendi (2142 4231/www.heritage
malta.org)*. **Open** 9am-5pm daily.
Admission €4.66; €2.33 reductions.

The Megalithic temple of Hagar Qim
lies on a windswept and rugged rock
plateau perched over the sea, and constitutes a single round structure with a
series of interconnected chambers of no
uniform size or shape. Furnishings are
limited to a couple of stone altars – the
'Fat Lady' statuettes of the ancient fertility cult that once worshipped here
are on display in the National Museum
of Archaeology (p55) – but simply
walking around it is enough to instil a
sense of the passing millennia.

Mnajdra Temples

*Qrendi (2142 4231/www.heritage
malta.org)*. **Open** 9am-5pm daily.
Admission €4.66; €2.33 reductions.

A short walk from Hagar Qim,
Mnajdra is one of the smallest and
most intimate of the major historical
temple groupings of Malta. It is also
one of the best preserved: several ceilings have collapsed in on its interior
chambers but the majority of walls
have survived. Like Hagar Qim,
detailed theories have been posited to
account for the astrological significance of the construction, with seasonal equinoxes and solstices bringing the
rays of the rising sun streaming into
the lower temple.

Mnajdra Temples

MALTA BY AREA

St Mary's Cathedral p126

Gozo & Comino

Victoria (Rabat)

It's a very pleasant 25-minute ferry trip or a ten-minute flight by seaplane to reach Gozo. The island is distinctly different in character from Malta – quieter, greener and with a simpler and more relaxed lifestyle. Many visitors choose to spend their entire holiday lapping up its tranquillity and charm, although most consider a day or two enough time to capture the essence of the island and to visit the main historical sights, the majority of which lie in the capital Victoria, also known as Rabat.

Here you'll find the Citadel, the hulking castle that constituted Gozo's first settlement and which was last rebuilt by the Knights in 1699. It remains a local landmark, set atop a hill overlooking the town and home to looming **St Mary's Cathedral** as well as four separate museums. Other attractions in Rabat include ornate **St George's Basilica** and numerous outdoor cafés in Independence Square, perfect places to break up a day's meandering around the arterial streets and looming Baroque townhouses of this intriguing city.

Sights & museums

Archaeology Museum

Mdina Gate Street, Citadel (2155 6144/www.heritagemalta.org). **Open** 9am-5pm daily. **Admission** €2.33; €0.58-€1.16 reductions. **Map** p124 C2 ❶
As a home for countless historical finds unearthed in Gozo and Comino over the years, the Archaeology Museum illustrates the development of the islands from prehistoric to early modern times. Oldest and most interesting are the

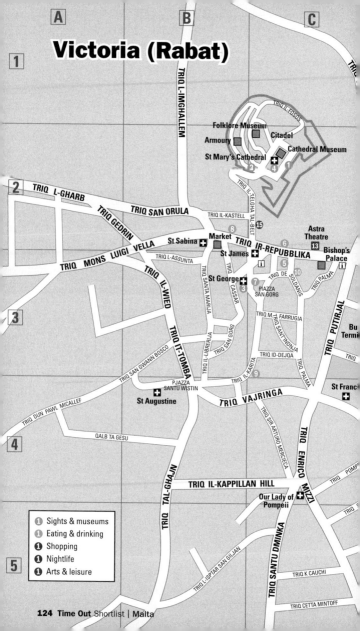

Victoria (Rabat)

Folklore Museum
Armoury
St Mary's Cathedral
Citadel
Cathedral Museum

TRIQ L-IMGHALLEM
TRIQ L-EDSOS
TRIQ IL-TELGHA TAL-BELT

TRIQ L-GHARB
TRIQ GEDRIN
TRIQ SAN ORULA
TRIQ IL-KASTELL

TRIQ MONS LUIGI VELLA
TRIQ L-ASSUNTA
St Sabina
Market
St James
TRIQ IR-REPUBBLIKA
Astra Theatre
Bishop's Palace

TRIQ IL-WIED
TRIQ SANTA MARIJA
St George
PIAZZA SAN GORG
TRIQ DE SOLDANIS
TRIQ PALMA

TRIQ IT-TOMBA
TRIQ IL-LIBRERIJA
TRIQ SAN GORG
CASSAR
TRIQ M. FARRUGIA
TRIQ SANT'INDNIJA
TRIQ PUTIRJAL
Bu Termi

TRIQ SAN GWANN BOSCO
TRIQ ID-DEJQA
TRIQ IL-KARTA
TRIQ

PJAZZA SANTU WISTIN
St Augustine
TRIQ VAJRINGA
St Franc

TRIQ DUN PAWL MICALLEF
QALB TA GESU

TRIQ TAL-GHAJN
TRIQ IL-KAPPILLAN HILL
TRIQ SIR ARTURO MERCIECA
TRIQ ENRICO MIZZI
TRIQ POMP

Our Lady of Pompeii
TRIQ

TRIQ SANTU DMINKA
TRIQ K CAUCHI

TRIQ L-ISPTAR SAN GILJAN
TRIQ CETTA MINTOFF

❶ Sights & museums
❶ Eating & drinking
❶ Shopping
❶ Nightlife
❶ Arts & leisure

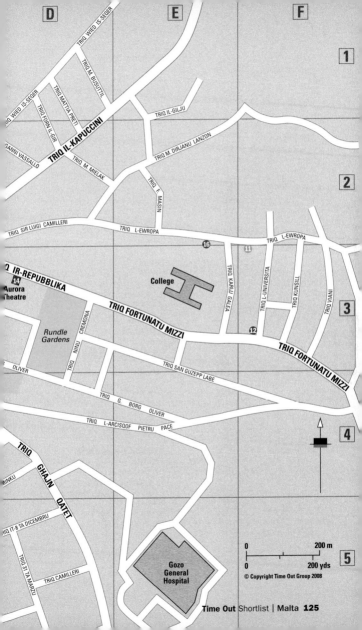

Neolithic and Bronze Age remains, mostly pottery and relics from the Ggantija Temples, then followed by Phoenician artefacts including a burial urn. The museum also displays amphorae and jewellery from the Roman period, while the Xlendi Room houses pieces from Greek and Roman wrecks recovered from the bay in 1961.

Old Prison

Cathedral Square, Citadel (2156 5988/www.heritagemalta.org). **Open** 9am-5pm daily. **Admission** €2.33, €0.58-€1.16 reductions. **Map** p124 C2 ➋
Originally connected to the adjoining Law Courts, this building served as a prison from the mid 16th until the early 20th century. The individual cells, branching off from a central courtyard, have been preserved right down to the graffiti covering the walls, which variously displays ships, handprints, games, animals and human figures, and provides an insight into the lives of inmates throughout the ages.

St George's Basilica

St George's Square (no phone). **Open** 7am-7pm daily. **Admission** free. **Map** p124 B3 ➌
This 17th-century basilica retains a medieval-style exterior dominated by two grand bell towers and a richly marbled Baroque interior with an elaborate altar and some outstanding works of art – most notably, four large paintings in the chancel depicting events from the life of St George, including a dramatic slaying of the dragon.

St Mary's Cathedral

Cathedral Square, Citadel (no phone). **Open** 9am-4.30pm daily. **Admission** €0.58. **Map** p124 C2 ➍
Designed in 1697 by the Maltese architect Lorenzo Gafa, St Mary's façade towers over the small square behind the Citadel's main gate. Gafa's looming bell tower makes good use of limited space (and dominates the skyline), but depleted parish funds meant that his planned dome was instead replaced with a convincing trompe l'oeil by the Italian artist Antonio Manuele.

Eating & drinking

Bellusa Café

34 Independence Square (2155 6243). **Open** 7am-7pm daily. No credit cards. **Café**. **Map** p124 C2 ➎
Coffee is served either in the refurbished townhouse interior or outdoors near the fish market, the latter an ideal location for people-watching amid the bustle of Independence Square. Good, inexpensive pizzas are also on offer alongside speciality pastizzi.

Café Jubilee

8 Independence Square (2155 8921/ www.cafejubilee.com). **Open** 8am-1am Mon-Thur, Sun; 8am-2am Fri, Sat. **Café**. **Map** p124 C3 ➏
With walls covered in curio prints, a wooden interior reminiscent of a British pub and decent Mediterranean food served all day, Gozo's original café-bar has spawned many imitators but is still leading the pack. It's quiet in the week, packed on weekends and has bracing pop music in the evenings.

Grapes

St George's Square (7947 3503). **Open** 8am-2am Mon-Thur; 8am-4am Fri-Sun. **Bar**. **Map** p124 C3 ➐
Outdoor seating in picturesque St George's Square makes this small, friendly wine bar a lovely place for early evening drinks with snacks of local antipasti. There's a good selection of wine on offer, but locals tend to opt for beer, and the place is often heaving with younger drinkers on weekends.

Maji Wine & Dine

6 Sir Adrian Dingli Street (2155 0878/www.majiwine-dine.com). **Open** 7-11pm Mon, Tue, Thur; 11.30am-2pm, 7-11pm Fri-Sun. €€. **Mediterranean**. **Map** p124 B2 ➑
A formerly struggling nightclub that has recently turned into a splendid, stylish restaurant in the heart of Gozo, with an upmarket interior, amiable owners, a great wine list and a highly imaginative menu featuring the likes of duck and courgette ravioli and pancetta-wrapped chicken roulade.

Gozo goes agro

Agrotourism: as ye sow, so shall ye reap.

Perhaps it's the diminutive size of most local farms, but the worldwide popularity of agrotourism had until recently eluded Malta. It was a bold step, then, for Victor Galea to introduce the concept to Gozo via the **Ager Foundation** (www. agerfoundation.com, 7901 7017), but one that is slowly changing the face of tourism on the island.

'The most important part of the programme is involving participants in the work itself,' says Victor, who personalises all the foundation's mostly day-long agrotourism adventures to cater to the specific tastes and preferences of his customers. As such, visitors can choose to do everything from milking sheep to picking and pickling capers, fishing in traditional Maltese boats or helping produce local cheeses and wines. Needless to say there are plenty of opportunities to reap the culinary rewards of the rustic life: days spent with local farmers will involve a traditional Gozitan lunch with the host's family, while those spent alongside fishermen will follow up an exhausting day

on the boat with a barbecue of the haul on the picturesque beaches of neighbouring Comino.

Nor does it need to be a case of back-breaking labour, with various physically demanding alternatives including hands-on tours of Gozo's archaeological sites, and tranquil bird watching expeditions during spring and autumn migrations. All of which makes for a great deal of outdoorsy fun, but there's also a serious side to the work done by the Ager Foundation – a non-governmental, non-profit organisation run by members of the Maltese Green Party (*ager* means 'field' in Latin).

The foundation aims to help develop the island's conomy while preserving its rural traditions and delicate ecosystems, with profits ploughed back into environmental aid work and rural development processes. All of which basically means that it's now possible to experience rural life in Gozo while taking something better than pictures away with you and leaving something far more valuable than footprints behind.

MALTA BY AREA

Dwejra

Il-Panzier

39 Charity Street (2155 9979). **Open** noon-2.30pm, 7-10pm daily. Closed last 3wks Dec. €€. **Italian**. Map p124 C3 ⑨
Beautifully located in a restored townhouse, Il-Panzier boasts wrought iron tables laid in a courtyard with a Sicilian lava floor and cascading fountain. The menu changes seasonally to make use of fresh ingredients, with typically Sicilian dishes including minced pork baked with milk and lots of herbs, as well as one of the best tiramisus across the islands.

Sopos Wine Bar

Independence Square (2155 0947). **Open** 9am-11pm daily. **Bar**. Map p124 C3 ⑩
Step back in time at this charming bar in Victoria's bustling main square, with pavement seating perfect for people-watching and a background symphony of birdsong from the tall trees overhead. Inside there are old wooden tables and either velvet armchairs or sofas to sink into, plus some great snacks on hand to soak up the wine.

It-Tmun Victoria

Europe Street (2156 6667). **Open** 6-10.30pm Mon-Wed, Fri, Sat; noon-2.30pm, 6-10.30pm Sun. €€. **Fusion**. Map p125 F3 ⑪

A formal setting and lush decor characterise one of Gozo's best restaurants, with abstract paintings by local artists and linen drapes providing seclusion for private functions. The menu ranges from Mediterranean delights – deep-fried ravioli, braised beef olives, grilled king prawns – to more Asian-inspired dishes, and the award-winning wine list is among the islands' finest. On top of all that, it's eminently affordable. **Other location** 3 Mount Carmel Street, Xlendi (2156 6276).

Shopping

Arkadia Commercial Centre

Fortunato Mizzi Street (2210 3000/www.arkadia.com.mt). **Open** *July-Sept* 9am-7pm daily. *Oct-June* 9am-1pm, 4-7pm Mon-Fri; 9am-7pm Sat. **Map** p125 F3 ⑫
A busy four-floor shopping centre with a large supermarket, a first floor big on branches of clothing companies like Morgan, Dorothy Perkins and Miss Sixty, and a second floor dedicated entirely to homeware.

Arts & leisure

Astra Theatre

9 Republic Street (2155 6256). **Tickets** €46.59-€58.23. **Map** p124 C2 ⑬

MALTA BY AREA

The Astra stages classical concerts and operas year round, with a programme of local acts interspersed with the occasional international star. The Maltese tenor Joseph Calleja is among the most famous performers to have played here.

Aurora Theatre

Republic Street (2156 2974). **Tickets** €5-€58. No credit cards. **Map** p125 D3 🔞
A large Baroque theatre featuring international touring plays and operas from November to May, along with occasional one-off events such as ballets and concerts from the Leone Philharmonic Orchestra.

Citadel Theatre

Castle Hill Street (2155 9955/www. citadelcinema.com). **Tickets** €3.14. **Map** p124 C2 🔞
Gozo's only cinema shows commercial Hollywood releases alongside a 30-minute tourist-oriented documentary on the island (every 30mins, 10.30am-4.30pm Mon-Sat; 10.30am-1pm Sun.

Gozo Sports Complex

Europe Street (2156 0678). **Open** 7am-9.45pm Mon-Fri; 8am-4.45pm Sat, Sun. **Map** p125 E2 🔞
A government-run sports complex with a good gym and the best basketball court on the islands. There are also squash, tennis, badminton and volleyball courts available for hire.

The Rest of Gozo & Comino

Beyond Rabat, the second largest concentration of Gozo's sights is in Xaghra. Its parish church towers over a public square that mixes colonial-era bars with contemporary restaurants, all of them with outdoor tables, while the town itself is home to the astonishing **Ggantija Temples**, still surprisingly intact despite their 5,600 years of accumulated history. Xaghra also has the well-preserved **Ta' Kola Windmill**,

now a museum, while coastal Calypso's Isle is alleged to have featured in Homer's *Odyssey* and is worth a visit for its ocean views.

In summer people tend to gather in the seaside resorts of Marsalforn and Xlendi: the former is an open bay lined with the island's single largest concentration of hotels and eateries, while smaller Xlendi is dramatically set in a gorge surrounded by sheer-drop coastal cliffs (although years of feverish development means it isn't half as pretty as it once was).

Yet more natural wonders lie west in the hilliest and least developed part of Gozo. Oceanside Dwejra is most notable for its oft-photographed Azure Window – a natural arch cut through a rocky peninsula – and is a fantastic place for scuba diving (see box p132). There are also decent beaches for more conventional swimming experiences dotted around the island: Ramla Bay is arguably the most popular (see box p114).

Also worth a detour is Gharb, best preserved of the island's old settlements, its streets teeming with ornate townhouses and with the fascinating **San Dimitri Chapel** and **Ta' Pinu Basilica** on its rural outskirts. Other notable areas around Gozo include Nadur, site of a bizarre annual festival (see box p34), the narrow, cliff-bound inlet of Mgarr, Qala with its various 18th-century windmills, and San Lawrenz, home to the unique **Ta' Dbiegi Crafts Centre**.

Comino, smallest of the three Maltese islands (it's inhabited by just four people), consists mainly of rock and shrub broken up by the lonely Comino Hotel and coastal St Mary's Tower, although the island's real attraction is the Blue Lagoon, a strip of turquoise water popular with boats and swimmers during summer.

MALTA BY AREA

Sights & museums

Ggantija Temples

Temple Street, Xaghra (2155 3194/ www.heritagemalta.org). **Open** 9am-5pm daily. **Admission** €3.49; €0.58-€1.75 reductions.

One of Malta's most important archaeological sites and the world's oldest freestanding building was erected around 3600 BC, composed of two temples and a series of chambers sharing an outer perimeter wall. The roofs have long since collapsed but the altars have survived along with faded spiral motifs framing the limestone passageways. Once used as a place of worship for the ancient fertility cult of the 'Fat Lady', the sheer scale of the temples (they would once have dominated the landscape for miles around) later led locals to believe they were erected by a race of giants, hence the name.

San Dimitri Chapel

Gharb (no phone). **Open** times vary. **Admission** free.

This isolated spot amid flat fields on the outskirts of Gharb once served as the setting for Malta's most famous legend. A widowed mother is said to have come to a chapel on this site and prayed for the intervention of St Demetrius after Muslims captured her

son; the saint then leaped out of the altar painting, galloped across the sea on his horse and brought the young man back. The present chapel, rebuilt in the 18th century, is a simple structure with a pitched roof and a single belfry, open erratically but well worth a visit all the same.

Ta' Kola Windmill

Windmill Street, Xaghra (2156 1071/ www.heritagemalta.org). **Open** 9am-5pm daily. **Admission** €2.33, €0.58-€1.16 reductions.

This beautiful stone windmill was built in 1725 and remained in operation until the mid 20th century. Today it serves as a museum, with full-scale reconstructions of carpenter's and blacksmith's workshops and a restored living quarters complete with kitchen and bedroom. You can climb the spiral staircase up to the tower supporting the sails for a closer look at the intricate wooden cogs that once powered the mill's grinding stones.

Ta' Pinu Basilica

Gharb (2155 6187). **Open** 7am-12.30pm, 1.30-7pm daily. **Admission** free.

Set in open countryside between Gharb and Ghasri, this church was built in the 1920s on the site of a chapel where Jesus is said to have appeared to a

Azure Window p129

MALTA BY AREA

Ta' Pinu Basilica

peasant in 1883, and it remains a place of pilgrimage to this day. The corridors leading to the chancel are cluttered with votive offerings, and the beautiful stone interior is embellished with carvings and sculptures by local craftsmen.

Xewkija Parish Church

St John the Baptist Square, Xewkija (no phone). **Open** 6am-noon, 4-7pm daily. **Admission** free.

The most recent church to be built in Gozo is also the largest, with the highest dome in Malta dominating the horizon for miles around. The structure's voluptuous Baroque edifice is shadowed by a single bell tower, while the interior has geometric floor tiling and enormous stone columns that lend an intimidating sense of scale.

Eating & drinking

Caffino

Hotel Calypso, Marsalforn Bay (2156 2000). **Open** 10am-midnight daily. **Café**.

The most popular café in Gozo serves fresh snacks either on its canopied alfresco terrace – framed with pot plants and views of fishermen at work – or within its bright, modern interior.

It's a popular haunt for Sunday afternoon teas thanks to its own-made brownies, chocolate cakes and fruit flans, and it also serves a mean cheese-or pea-filled pastizzi.

Country Terrace

Zewwieq Street, Mgarr (2155 0248/ www.country-terrace.com). **Open** *Apr-Oct* noon-3pm, 6.30-11pm daily. *Nov-Mar* noon-3pm, 6.30-11pm Tue-Sun. **€€**. **Mediterranean**.

Simple, hearty food in a welcoming restaurant with magnificent terrace views of Mgarr Harbour and the spectacular Blue Lagoon of Comino. The menu is big on fresh fish dishes and rabbit is cooked the traditional way in red wine and garlic.

Gesther's

8th September Avenue, Xaghra (2155 6621). **Open** noon-2.30pm Mon-Sat. **€**. **Maltese**.

Two sisters run this small, informal eatery with fixed Formica tables. Gozitan home cooking is the name of the game, from rustic soups and traditional fish pies to chicken baked in stock with potatoes and onions, all of it delicious and enormously filling despite costing next to nothing.

That sinking feeling

Flippers are the footwear of choice for underwater tourists.

Malta and Gozo are increasingly popular diving destinations thanks to their natural geological features and the fantastic array of wrecks awaiting more intrepid explorers.

Among the finest local formations is the breathtaking **Blue Hole**, lying at the bottom of the picturesque Azure Window in Dwejra, Gozo: swim through the hole and look back to see light filtering through in shimmering hues of cyan and sapphire. The water subsequently becomes very deep, with some interesting marine life loitering around 40 metres (130 feet) below sea level. Equally stunning is the **Double Arch** at Gozo's Xwejni Bay, where divers can swim between a pair of undersea arches, with high visibility and plenty of ancient shark teeth scattered over the seabed.

A range of local wrecks are equally well positioned for both beginners (the **HMS Maori** lies a mere 13 metres/43 feet beneath the water's surface in Valletta) and the downright adventurous alike (the appropriately named **HMS Stubborn** is 53 metres/ 174 feet beneath the waters off Qawra), although perhaps Malta's finest wreck is the enormous **Um el Faroud**, which sank a few years ago after an explosion rocked the Malta dockyard. Marine life surrounding the wreck is abundant, visibility tends to be excellent and the site became twice as interesting in 2007 when a severe storm split the vessel into two. Finally, the compact **Rozi Tugboat** off of Cirkewwa – lying around 30 metres (98 feet) beneath the point where the Gozo ferries depart – offers a dive with sensational visibility and a vivid show of colourful wildlife including octopuses, barracudas and eels.

The majority of Maltese dive schools provide Professional Association of Diving Instructor (PADI) courses, while some also offer qualifications approved by the British Sub Aqua Club (BSAC). An advanced open water course, sufficient for most recreational diving requirements, costs around €420 and takes about five days to complete. Introductory dives for complete novices are also available for about €30 to €35. For those visitors who have already qualified, accompanied dives in Malta cost from around €23 each including the rental of cylinders and weights, making them among the cheapest in the world.

Jeffrey's

10 Gharb Street, Gharb (2156 1006).
Open *Apr-Oct* 6-10.30pm Mon-Sat.
€€. Mediterranean.
Jeffrey's serves competent traditional dishes such as rabbit in wine and garlic alongside more wide-ranging concoctions such as beef pancakes and excellent steaks in either a mushroom or pepper sauce. The charming townhouse location also has a small courtyard, although winter sees the place closed up so the sun-loving owner can flee to the warmer side of the globe.

Il-Kartell

Marina Street, Marsalforn (2155 6918/www.il-kartell.com). **Open** *Jan, Feb* 6-11pm Fri, Sat. *Mar-May* noon-3.30pm, 6-11pm Tue, Thur-Sun. *June-Oct* noon-3.30pm, 6-11pm Mon, Tue, Thur-Sun; 6-11pm Wed. *Nov, Dec* noon-3.30pm Mon, Tue, Thur; noon-3.30pm, 6-11pm Fri-Sun. **€€. Mediterranean**.
Fantastic yet informal Mediterranean eating here starts with the likes of pickled tuna antipasto or hearty fish soup before moving on to mains of meat, grilled fish or pasta (penne with Maltese sausage, sun-dried tomatoes and pickled Gozo cheese is a winner). The outside terrace is packed in the warmer months thanks to its charming waterside seating, so book ahead.

Il-Kcina tal-Barrakka

28 Manoel de Vilhena Street, Mgarr (2155 6543). **Open** 7.30-10.30pm Tue-Sun. Closed Nov-Apr. **€€€**. No credit cards. **Mediterranean**.
Many Maltese locals travel purposely to Gozo simply for a meal at Il-Kcina tal-Barrakka. It's among the island's best eateries thanks to its excellent food (you'll struggle to find fresher fish) and the Mediterranean spirit lent by its pretty harbourside location and warm, familial atmosphere in which everyone seems to know everyone else.

Mgarr Ix-Xini Kiosk

Mgarr Ix-Xini Bay, Xewkija (2155 0208). **Open** *June-Sept* 10.30am-11pm daily. *Mar-May, Oct* 10.30am-5pm daily (fine weather only). **€. Maltese**.
Chicken, lamb and pork are also served, but it's the fresh fish, simply grilled and served with chips and salad, that provides the main draw at this small, nameless eatery with a number of outdoor tables on the stony shore of a scenic fjord.

Oleander

10 Victory Square, Xaghra (2155 7230). **Open** noon-3pm, 7-10.30pm Tue-Sun. **€€. Maltese**.
Oleander's menu is big on locally inspired dishes such as fried rabbit glazed with home-made red wine sauce, roast local lamb and goat's cheese ravioli in a rich tomato sauce. Plainly grilled meat and fish mains are also popular at this quaint restaurant with cosy outdoor seating, perfect for people-watching in the town square.

Otters

St Mary Road, Marsalforn (2156 2473). **Open** noon-5pm, 7-11pm daily. **€€**. **Mediterranean**.
A brilliant seaside location, great food and amicable owners have made Otters a local favourite, plus a recent cosmetic overhaul has lent it a stylish contemporary interior in striking grey and white. Fish dishes include pasta with clams in white wine, lightly seared tuna steaks and charcoal-grilled swordfish, all twice as tasty when eaten on the terrace with its views of the open ocean and its soundtrack of gently lapping waves.

Ta' Frenc

Marsalforn Road, Xaghra (2155 3888/www.tafrencrestaurant.com). **Open** *Apr-Dec* noon-1.30pm, 7-10pm Mon, Wed-Sun. *Jan-Mar* noon-2.30pm, 7-10pm Fri, Sat; noon-2.30pm Sun. **€€€€. Mediterranean**.
Decorated with local art and traditional Maltese clocks, Ta' Frenc is as classy as it is cosy, but it's the food that makes it Gozo's real 'don't miss' dining destination. The seasonal menu is outstanding, from simply fried fish with roasted vegetables to more elaborate dishes such as rabbit with pear and liver stuffing. And what goes into the kitchen is

MALTA BY AREA

as impressive as the stuff that comes out of it: most herbs on the menu are grown in the garden and most game reared by the owners themselves, while own-label champagne and white wine is specifically blended for Ta' Frenc by prestigious French vineyards.

Ta' Pawlu
4 Manoel de Vilhena Street, Mgarr (2155 8355). **Open** 6.30-10pm Mon, Wed-Sat; noon-2.30pm, 6.30-10pm Sun. **€€. Mediterranean**.
A small restaurant charmingly decorated and with tables spilling on to a tiny outdoor terrace in a former boatyard. Ta' Pawlu features a menu of simply cooked fresh fish alongside superb specials such as calamari cooked in fresh herbs, garlic and wine, or veal and ham tossed in mint and flour, fried and served with a delicate white wine reduction.

Tatita's Restaurant
34 San Lawrenz Square, San Lawrenz (2156 6482). **Open** Mar-Oct noon-3.30pm, 6-10.30pm daily. **€€€. Mediterranean**.
Tatita's is known for serving hearty, incredibly fresh Mediterranean dishes in a delightful interior – set in a beautifully preserved townhouse embellished with striking contemporary features – or on its pleasant outdoor terrace in the bustling town square. Service tends to be excellent and extremely friendly at this informal, family-run restaurant.

Ta' Vestru
5 St Joseph Square, Qala (2155 9090). **Open** 11.30am-3pm, 5.30pm-midnight Tue-Sun. **€. Maltese**.
The affordability of hearty Maltese food at Ta' Vestru never fails to amaze visitors, with delicious Gozitan pizzas with a variety of toppings (local cheese features on most combinations) for less than €5, and bottles of house wine for not much more. This is a quaint, simple eaterie, justifiably popular with locals thanks to its lovely location in front of Qala's parish church, although service is rather slow.

It-Tmun Xlendi
3 Mount Carmel Street, Xlendi (2156 6276). **Open** noon-2.30pm, 6-10pm Mon, Wed-Sun. **€€. Fusion**.
One of the best and most solidly established restaurants in Gozo, the Xlendi branch of It-Tmun is wonderfully decorated with a nautical theme and has outdoor tables for laid-back summer dining. The remarkable menu boasts a confident mix of seasonal French food alongside rustic Mediterranean meals (grilled fish and seafood is a speciality) and even Asian-inspired dishes.
Other location Europe Street, Victoria (2156 6667).

Shopping

Ta' Dbiegi Crafts Centre
Frangisk Portelli Street, San Lawrenz (2155 3722). **Open** June-Sept 9.30am-6pm daily. Oct-May 9am-4.30pm daily.
A cluster of artisan workshops producing and selling locally made crafts including candles, ceramics, lace, leatherwork, brassware and blown glass. Whether you're looking for Maltese-themed home decor or just a neat souvenir, this is the place to come. The selection is extensive and the quality tends to be excellent, plus the centre has been recently upgraded thanks to significant EU funding.

Nightlife

La Grotta
Xlendi (2155 1149/www.lagrotta leisure.com). **Open** May-Oct 10pm-4am Sat. **Admission** €4.66.
An outstanding open-air club sprawling down the Xlendi valley and lighting up the surrounding rock drops and abundant vegetation. Its stunning backdrop and unique location (the dancefloor is set in a cave, hence the name) make this one of the most unusual clubbing venues around, with a playlist that lurches from progressive house to techno and pulls in big name DJs like David Guetta, Ritchie Hawtin and Mr C. La Grotta also hosts the annual MTV Summer Dance event.

MALTA BY AREA

Essentials

Fortina Spa Resort p145

Hotels

Mention a holiday in Malta in the 1970s or '80s and you would have most likely conjured up images of faceless concrete blocks filled with sunburned package tourists or family-run guesthouses catering for elderly history boffins.

Not any more. In the last 15 years a raft of five-star openings has changed the landscape of Maltese tourism, offering guests the option of a stay so luxurious that it wouldn't look out of place in Dubai. Many such places pitch themselves more as self-contained resorts than hotels per se – the **Westin Dragonara Resort** or the recently extended **Hilton Malta** in Paceville, for example, the latter set in the swanky Portomaso marina complex and offering no less than four swimming pools (three of them outdoors) alongside a range of bars, restaurants and fitness facilities; or the **Fortina Spa Resort** in Sliema, which includes four separate spas featuring everything from saunas and steam rooms to acupuncture, Ayuverda and 'crystal sound therapy'. Such places have also come to dominate the traditional package tourist destinations of the northwestern beach resorts, with the **Radisson SAS Golden Sands Resort & Spa** in Mellieha offering a private sandy beach and a wide range of gourmet eating options in a coastal town founded on beach loungers and banana boat rides.

All of which is well and good for those determined to live like lords of the island, but there are still decent budget options available – the **Hotel Castille** in central

ESSENTIALS

Valletta, for example, or the **Comfort Inn** in Sliema – plus a range of places like the **Gillieru Harbour Hotel** catering to those seeking more traditional seaside holidays with a close proximity to both the sand and the tourist strip.

Those looking to stay on the sister island of Gozo will also find various hotels covering all corners of the spectrum, from the budget **Electra Hotel** and the more isolated **Hotel Ta' Cenc** to the smart **Kempinski San Lawrenz Resort**. Comino, meanwhile, has just one hotel – the appropriately-named **Comino Hotel**, open from April to October only.

Valletta

British Hotel
40 Battery Street (2122 4730/ www.britishhotel.com). **€**.
The British Hotel offers conveniently located but rather basic en suite rooms with beautiful tiling but otherwise stark furniture and decor. Some rooms have air conditioning for an extra charge and the best rooms are at the front, where majestic views of the Grand Harbour will set you back a very reasonable €4.66 extra per day.

Excelsior Grand Hotel
NEW *Great Siege Road, Floriana (2125 0520/www.excelsior.com.mt).* **€€€€**.
It's virtually brand new, but something about the Excelsior's wall-to-wall carpeting and abundance of stained wood furnishings makes it seem strangely old fashioned. Nor will the guiding aesthetic of its interior design (it's supposed to resemble a cruise liner) please all comers. And yet, for all that, the hotel is extremely well situated – just a five-minute walk from Valletta – and is only the second hotel on the islands to offer its guests a private marina. Extensive conference facilities include a ballroom seating around 950 people, plus there's a spa, a (very) small gym and indoor and outdoor pools.

SHORTLIST

Best for luxury
- Hilton Malta (p142)
- InterContinental (p142)
- Westin Dragonara Resort (p145)

Best for families
- Ramla Bay Resort (p147)
- RIU Seabank & Spa (p148)
- Suncrest Hotel (p148)

Best for a secluded sojourn
- Corinthia Palace Hotel & Spa (p147)
- Hotel Comino (p148)
- Hotel Ta' Cenc (p150)

Best for old world charm
- Le Méridien Phoenicia (p139)
- Xara Palace Relais & Chateaux (p146)

Best for beach access
- Dolmen Resort Hotel (p147)
- Radisson SAS Golden Sands Resort & Spa (p147)
- Riviera Resort & Spa (p148)

Best for party animals
- Corinthia San Gorg (p139)
- Downtown Hotel (p150)
- Golden Tulip Vivaldi (p142)

Best for dining in style
- Fortina Spa Resort (p145)
- Hotel Juliani (p142)
- Le Méridien St Julian's (p143)

Best for shopaholics
- Marina Hotel (p145)
- Osborne Hotel (p139)
- Preluna Hotel & Spa (p146)

Best on a budget
- Comfort Inn (p145)
- Electra Hotel (p150)
- Hotel Castille (p139)

Best spas
- Kempinski San Lawrenz Resort (p150)
- San Antonio Hotel & Spa (p148)

ESSENTIALS

www.treesforcities.org

Trees for Cities
Charity registration number 1032154

Travelling creates so many
lasting memories.

Make your trip mean something for
years to come - not just for you but
for the environment and for people
living in deprived urban areas.

Anyone can offset their flights,
but when you plant trees with
Trees for Cities, you'll help create
a green space for an urban
community that really needs it.

To find out more visit
www.treesforcities.org

Leave
Your
Mark

Create a green future for cities.

Grand Harbour Hotel

St Ursula Street (2124 6003/ www.grandharbourhotel.com). €.

A well-located seven-storey townhouse that's been converted into a budget hotel popular with backpackers, offering a range of rather spartan double rooms with bathrooms and functional aluminium balconies, and some with air conditioning as extra. Rooms at the front have views of the Grand Harbour, and the main shopping streets of Valletta are just a short walk away.

Hotel Castille

Castille Square (2124 3677/ www.hotelcastillemalta.com). €.

The bright, well-aired rooms at the Hotel Castille boast air conditioning, en suite bathrooms, televisions and telephones, and the Baroque building in which it is housed is furnished with grand staircases and wide corridors. The hotel is well located between the Auberge de Castille and Upper Barrakka Gardens, and just a short walk around the corner from the many shops and restaurants of central Valletta. The hotel also houses two restaurants: a more formal rooftop eaterie and one in the barrel-vaulted cellar serving pizzas and pasta dishes.

Le Méridien Phoenicia

The Mall, Floriana (2122 5241/ www.malta.lemeridien.com). €€€€.

One of the oldest hotels in Malta, Le Méridien Phoenicia is still a force to be reckoned with when it comes to accommodation across the island. The interior decoration of the vast, elegantly vaulted lobby conjures up the prestige of a bygone era, while its seven acres of landscaped gardens offer guests a wonderful place to unwind with the bastions of the capital still looming above them. The rooms are spacious and smartly decorated, and have fantastic views of both the lavish gardens and Marsamxett Harbour beyond. On top of all that, the hotel's location couldn't be more useful, a short walk from the city walls and a few metres from the main bus terminal.

Osborne Hotel

South Street (2124 3656/ www.osbornehotel.com). €€€.

The Osborne is a relatively large and rather old-fashioned hotel, the subject of a recent refurbishment but still clinging gracefully to its antiquated charm and intimacy. Don't expect anything grand: its range of plain double rooms are decorated with plain varnished furniture and equipped with air conditioning, telephones and televisions, but are nothing to write home about in terms of aethetics. Still, it's a friendly, functional place in the heart of Valletta, just a few minutes' walk away from the shopping strip of Republic Street.

St Julian's & Paceville

Corinthia Marina

St George's Bay, St Julian's (2138 1719/www.corinthiahotels.com). €€€.

As a three-star version of its local sister hotel the Corinthia San Gorg (see below), the Corinthia Marina trades a certain amount of grandeur for a more modern, minimalist approach. The spacious rooms are decorated in true Mediterranean style with wrought iron beds and tiled floors, and there is a range of excellent restaurants to choose from, all of them on the water's edge, so one never really needs to leave if lethargy suddenly strikes.

Corinthia San Gorg

St George's Bay, St Julian's (2137 4111/www.corinthiahotels.com). €€€.

The summery yellow and blue interior of the Corinthia San Gorg complements the golden sunlight streaming through its large windows and the clear blue of both sea and sky beyond them. Very clean, tastefully decorated and with supremely friendly staff, the hotel also boasts a great location – a few minutes' walk from the bustle of Paceville's clubs and bars, but not so close as to be disturbed by them when they kick out of an evening. A number of the rooms have been recently refurbished.

Wanted.
Jumpers, coats and people with their knickers in a twist.

From the people who feel moved to bring us their old books and CDs, to the people fed up to the back teeth with our politicians' track record on climate change, Oxfam supporters have one thing in common. They're passionate. If you've got a little fire in your belly, we'd love to hear from you. Visit us at **oxfam.org.uk**

Be Humankind (⦵) **Oxfam**

Registered charity No. 202918

Boutique and the beast

The Hotel Juliani offers peace amid the partying.

Balancing proximity to Paceville's bustle of bars and clubs with a quaint hotel not constantly assaulted by noise is no mean feat, but salvation comes in the form of Malta's first and only boutique option, the four-star **Hotel Juliani** (p142).

The hotel's old-fashioned townhouse façade hides an ultra-modern interior, from the clean lines and glass furnishings of the informal lobby to the rooms themselves – tastefully decorated in deep browns and blues, and with free Wi-Fi, luxury whirlpool baths and double-glazed balconies overlooking the bay – to the rooftop pool and adjoining terrace, site of a smart cocktail bar in summer.

'Malta has plenty of faceless five-star resorts and more than enough budget accommodation for package tourists,' says Georgios Rouvelas, operations manager at the Juliani. 'We wanted to create somewhere with real character, designed to dazzle the senses but make guests feel welcome at the same time. We wanted a hotel that felt like a very special home.'

Nor is it just a hotel. Many of its patrons are locals who come to sip coffee on the terrace of the ground floor Café Juliani – its sprawling views over Spinola Bay blighted, in the opinion of some, only by Richard England's controversial *Love* sculpture – or the Maltese businessmen who retreat into the cool of the bar area to discuss mergers over a beer and a peppery tuna and *gbejna* cheese salad. There are more satisfying eating options upstairs, including the laid-back Joia restaurant – where head chef Giuseppe puts two decades of pizza-making to work – and Asian fusion eaterie Zest (p80), boasting a menu that straddles East (steamed red snapper in a Thai curry sauce) and West (seared salmon topped with fois gras and served on a bed of truffle mash).

All of which makes the proximity of Paceville's bars and clubs a distinct advantage that you may never indulge in. After all, why go out for hamburger when you can have seared salmon at home?

Golden Tulip Vivaldi

Dragonara Road, St Julian's (2137 8100/www.goldentulipvivaldi.com). €€. There's as much of a musical theme as you'd expect at a hotel with 'Vivaldi' in its name – from the classically inspired lobby to the musically oriented works of art on the walls – but the composer himself would probably turn in his grave at the sound of the upbeat house anthems floating over from nearby Paceville's muddle of Brit-packer clubs and bars. Luckily, the Golden Tulip Vivaldi's rooms all have full double-glazing, but it's still probably worth looking elsewhere if you're after a family or romantic break. That said, those seeking an affable, affordable base in the heart of Malta's nightlife scene need look no further.

Hilton Malta

Portomaso, St Julian's (2138 3383/ www.malta.hilton.com). €€€€.

The Hilton has been sumptuously designed to overlook both the award-winning man-made yacht marina of Portomaso and the sprawling sea beyond it, a vista that can also be enjoyed from any one of the three pools in its stylish outdoor recreation area. Rooms are simple but extremely elegant, with a distinct Mediterranean touch, while exhibitions by local artists regularly lend a splash of colour to the bustling lobby. A number of decent hotel restaurants offer to take guests on a gastronomic tour from Thailand and Japan to the Mediterranean.

Hotel Juliani

12 St George's Road, St Julian's (2138 8000/www.hoteljuliani.com). €€. See box p141.

InterContinental

St George's Bay, St Julian's (2137 7600/www.ichotelsgroup.com). €€€€.

ESSENTIALS

The largest five-star hotel on the island isn't built on the water's edge like so many of its competitors, but more than makes up for its inland location with its own private sandy beach (the only one of its kind), a few minutes' walk away and open to anyone staying at the hotel. Guests may also relax at the in-house beauty studio (9.30am-7pm Mon-Sat), a tranquil haven of soothing music and flickering candlelight that offers all manner of beauty therapies – from facials and manicures to professional massages. Rooms are large and lavish and tastefully decorated with warm bronze fittings, and feel naturally cool even in summer. It's one of the priciest places to stay locally, but one of the most opulent by a long way.

Le Méridien St Julian's

39 Main Street, Balluta Bay, St Julian's (2311 2104/www.starwoodhotels.com/lemeridien). €€€€.

Art plays an important role at Le Méridien St Julian's, from the internal décor – home to art deco influences and with walls featuring paintings by local artists – to the architectural design of the building itself. The hotel also pleases its fair share of more gastronomically inclined guests, with cuisine courtesy of Michelin two-star head chef Michel Rostang. More avid shoppers, meanwhile, will find a number of boutique stores on the ground floor.

Radisson SAS Bay Point Resort

St George's Bay, St Julian's (2134 7894/www.radissonsas.com). €€€€.
The Radisson SAS Bay Point Resort combines luxurious, spacious and sleek rooms with a range of superb facilities, including free Wi-Fi, indoor and outdoor pools, a beauty salon and three restaurants of varying expense and culinary intensity. But it's the

Le Méridien Phoenicia p139

ESSENTIALS

Westin Dragonara Resort

hotels' proximity to the water's edge that really makes it stand out from the pack: all 252 rooms boast balconies with the clear blue Mediterranean lapping almost directly beneath them. You'll struggle to find a more opulent base in the St Julian's area.

Westin Dragonara Resort

Dragonara Road, St Julian's (2138 1000/www.westinmalta.com). €€€€.

Occupying the largest landscaped grounds in all of St Julian's, this neo-classical multi-storey hotel has an impressive range of facilities, including a large outdoor pool, a well-equipped fitness centre also popular with locals, various quality restaurants, a shopping complex and even an on-site casino. Its coral and cream façade is particularly striking and overlooks the sea, while the large, bright rooms are fully equipped with grand bathrooms and a good range of luxurious amenities.

Sliema

Comfort Inn

29 Cathedral Street (2133 4221/ www.comfortinnmalta). €.
No credit cards.

A large townhouse converted into a family-run guesthouse with 12 bedrooms, hardly the most stylish pad around but perfect for budget travellers not wanting to compromise on a central location. The spacious lounge is brimming with books and information on local tours and sights, and there is also a communal TV area shared by guests. The simple bedrooms on the upper floor come as singles, doubles or family rooms that can sleep four, and all have en suite bathrooms.

Fortina Spa Resort

Tigné Seafront (2346 0000/ www.hotelfortina.com). €€€€.

Guests find themselves immersed in a world of pure luxury at the Fortina Spa Resort, where the lush 35sq m bedrooms offer splendid views of either the hotel's landscaped garden or the lush blue of the Mediterranean. The usual facilities are complemented by some truly luxurious touches, from four on-site spas, an enormous outdoor pool and a decent fitness centre to a range of restaurants including Taste (see p96). For those looking to splash out, there are bedrooms offering personalised spa treatments, nine of them also with a private roof garden and pool.

Imperial Hotel

Rudolph Street (2134 4093/www. imperialhotelmalta.com). €€.

Live life in the pink at the Imperial Hotel, where the walls, columns and even the parasols perched beside the rooftop pool are a distinct shade of salmon. The hotel is set in an imposing building with grand staircases, ornate ceiling murals and a spacious lobby replete with antique furnishings. There's also a good selection of on-site facilities including a restaurant, bar, games room and charming gardens, buzzing with activity in the mornings but suitably relaxing as the sun goes down. Rooms are large and comfortable, and boast en suite bathrooms, air conditioning, televisions and telephones, and the shop-lined promenade of Sliema is a ten-minute walk away.

Marina Hotel

Tigné Seafront (2133 6461/www. themarinahotelsliema.com). €€.

If you're looking to stay in a central location for a price that won't break the bank, then the Marina Hotel could well be ideal. Located right in the heart of Sliema's bustling shopping and café district, the hotel has recently been refurbished: the rooms are comfortable and functional, with €9.32 extra per person bringing balconies with one of the most beautiful views on the island – a sweeping vista of Marsamxett Harbour and Valletta. There's a small jacuzzi on the roof, but no pool; visitors instead have free access to a nearby lido.

Palace

NEW *Triq Il-Kbira (2262 3202/ www.thepalacesliemahotel.com).* €€€€.

ESSENTIALS

With ample conference facilities, this new five-star hotel in the heart of Sliema tends to cater to corporate clients. Artfully designed to within an inch of its life, highlights include a breathtaking infinity pool on the roof complete with 360° views across Malta, a large spa and fitness centre, and six themed designer suites – the sound-proofed music suite, for example, comes equipped with a drum kit and a personalised rock PA system. The Temptations rooftop restaurant serves creative Asian fusion cuisine, while the main Tabloid restaurant offers buffet breakfasts and divine a la carte dinners. There's also a café-bar on the ground floor serving everything from sandwiches to three course meals and open all day to guests and non-guests.

Preluna Hotel & Spa
Tower Road (2133 4001/ www.preluna-hotel.com). €€.
The Preluna Hotel & Spa has a fantastic location right in the heart of one of Sliema's main shopping strips; it's also a stone's throw from the sea – access to which is from a rocky beach nearby – and boasts its own lido. Rooms are bright and airy and the best among them have stunning ocean views, while the fitness centre has recently been given a facelift and is now frequented by as many locals as guests. There's also a lovely spa equipped with a swimming pool, jacuzzi, sauna and steam room, plus professional massage and beauty therapy studios.

Victoria Hotel
Gorg Borg Olivier Street (2133 4711/www.victoriahotel.com). €€€.
An elegant Victorian-inspired hotel with comfortable rooms featuring the usual amenities (including air conditioning) and small balconies. The hotel lobby is a wonderful place to loiter, large and littered with comfortable sofas, a fireplace and dark wood furnishings. In an amusing throwback to the colonial era, the hotel's halls are named after such notable British luminaries as Lords Tennyson and Byron,

while the Sir Walter Scott Terrace offers alfresco dining opportunities in more temperate weather.

Waterfront Hotel
The Strand, Gzira (2133 3434/www. waterfronthotelmalta.com). €€.
A tastefully understated, artfully modern and eminently comfortable hotel with a charming, nautically themed lobby, situated as close to the watery fringe of Sliema as its name implies. The bright, clean and well-sized rooms have en suite bathrooms, air conditioning and a good range of the usual amenities, and some enjoy superb views across the harbour to Valletta. The Regatta Restaurant offers smart terrace dining, plus there's also a more informal pizzeria for those guests not wanting to stand on ceremony.

Mdina & Rabat

Point De Vue Guesthouse
2-7 Saqqajja Square, Rabat (2145 4117/www.pointdevuemalta.com). €.
This erstwhile Rabat townhouse has been converted into a no-frills guesthouse with 12 rooms – some single, some twin – all of them rather spartan in terms of interior design and sporting furnishings that are modern but dormitory dull. That said, prices are cheap enough to allow guests to overlook stylistic issues, and there are two restaurants – Butcher's Grill and the more informal Java Lounge and Terrace – both with superb sea views.

Xara Palace Relais & Chateaux
Council Square, Mdina (2145 0560/ www.xarapalace.com.mt). €€€.
This charming hotel couldn't ask for a more dramatic location, set in the historic central square of Mdina and with a grand Baroque interior based around a court now serving as a lobby. Rooms are luxurious: the best of them take advantage of the city's hilltop location to offer views encompassing the entire sweep of northern Malta; others are equipped with personal jacuzzis. The

rooftop De Mondion Restaurant offers superb French cuisine with the hustle and bustle of the ancient city as an atmospheric backdrop (p108).

The Rest of Malta

Coastline Hotel

Salina Bay, Salina (2157 3781). €€.
Set in a suitably quiet location on the outskirts of town, the Coastline Hotel is around a half hour walk from the touristy stretch of St Paul's Bay – great news for those seeking relative peace and quiet as well as sun, sea and sand. The a la carte La Costa restaurant caters for those who'd rather avoid buffet dinners, while the enormous hotel grounds include an outdoor pool with terrace and rambling gardens, and many of the clean, functional rooms have sea views for an extra charge. There's also nightly entertainment of the old-fashioned beach resort variety.

Corinthia Palace Hotel & Spa

De Paule Avenue, Balzan (2144 0301/ www.corinthia.com). €€€.
A large hotel set in sprawling, landscaped grounds and with a range of excellent restaurants, among them the popular Rickshaw restaurant and sushi bar, the upmarket Villa Corinthia and the alfresco Poolside eaterie. There's also a wonderful spa, a large outdoor swimming pool and tennis courts, while the rooms are all large, bright and cheerfully decorated. The hotel's location in the quiet village of Balzan makes it ideal for those hoping to avoid the hustle and bustle of more touristy corners of the island, but less so for those looking to spend the majority of their time on the beach or in the town centre (Valletta is roughly a 20-minute bus ride away).

Dolmen Resort Hotel

Dolmen Street, Qawra, (2355 2355/ www.dolmen.com.mt). €€.
One of Bugibba's largest hotels, the Dolmen is a sprawling outfit with a mind-boggling range of facilities, including a private lido, a popular nightclub and a casino. There are also restaurants, pool bars and wine bars aplenty, and most of the rooms have a balcony overlooking the sea – which, as you'd expect, is a stone's throw away. Corporate clients make up a large proportion of visitors, but the spacious interconnecting family bedrooms are ideal for those with children.

Gillieru Harbour Hotel

Church Street, St Paul's Bay (2157 2720/www.gillieru.com). €€.
Small and basic but with bright rooms that feel naturally cool, even in the height of summer, the Gillieru Harbour Hotel is an affordable option for those seeking a slice of the action of touristy St Paul's Bay. Most rooms have small balconies that offer sweeping vistas of the bay itself, and there's a decent seafood restaurant on the ground floor.

Radisson SAS Golden Sands Resort & Spa

Golden Bay, Mellieha (2356 1000/ www.radissonsas.com). €€€€.
Dramatically located on a cliff edge overlooking the gently lapping shore, the recently established Radisson SAS Golden Sands Resort & Spa offers stunning sea or country views from every one of its 337 tastefully decorated rooms and suites. The extensive hotel spa is well equipped to make an indulgent break of even the most fleeting visit, as are the various bars and restaurants – Essence (p113) is one of the finest gourmet eateries on the island – plus there's free Wi-Fi throughout. On top of that, the hotel's access to Malta's most beautiful sandy beaches is unparalleled.

Ramla Bay Resort

Marfa, Mellieha (2281 2281/ www.ramlabayresort.com). €€€.
The Ramla Bay Resort lays claim to a great deal of sprawling land, offering those seeking solitude the chance to unwind in the shade of countless bamboo parasols, read a book on any number of landscaped terraces or sip a

ESSENTIALS

cocktail as the sun sets beyond the watery horizon. There's a heated indoor pool in winter, while more temperate months see guests take to the lagoon-style outdoor pool. The resort is a great choice for families, with kids' play areas and activities and plenty of tailored family rooms, plus there's a decent bar and restaurant, an internet café and souvenir shops on site.

RIU Seabank & Spa

Marfa Road, Mellieha (2152 1460/ www.seabankhotel.com). €€.

You're guaranteed a sea view at this hotel, which is well suited to families thanks to its nightly entertainment and range of kids' amenities including an activity club and a playhouse. The indoor and outdoor pools are both fantastic – the latter curling around the front of the building like a lagoon – while a number of restaurants and bars cater to both quick bites and formal sit-down dinners. Beach bums will be pleased at the proximity of Mellieha Bay's seemingly endless sands, a short walk away; more indulgent holidaymakers can pamper themselves with treatments and massages; and adventurous types can partake in sporting activities – water-based and otherwise – organised by the hotel.

Riviera Resort & Spa

Marfa Bay, Mellieha (2152 5900/ www.riviera.com.mt). €€.

The Riviera Resort and Spa's location on the northernmost tip of the island means that it has very few neighbours and is bathed in glorious sunshine all day long. Huge windows make the lobby a great place to idle away the afternoon with a book, chat with friends or simply admire the breathtaking views over Gozo and Comino, and there's a range of rooms to suit all visitors, including rooms tailored to disabled guests and family rooms joined with connecting doors. Corporate clients are well catered for with various meeting rooms, plus there's a spa and a selection of bars and restaurants, many with stylish terraces.

San Antonio Hotel & Spa

Tourists Street, Qawra (2158 3434/ www.sanantonio-malta.com). €€€.

Whitewashed walls, well-aired rooms and an enormous, eye-catching limestone relief in the lobby all give the San Antonio Hotel & Spa a typically Mediterranean look and feel. The resort lays claim to its own private (rocky) beach, plus a range of facilities that includes three pools (one indoor, one outdoor, one for kids), two saunas, a comprehensive spa and wellness centre and a range of eating and drinking options – from the formal Costa restaurant and the Bonaparte Brasserie to the laid-back pool bar – plus there's live entertainment every night.

Suncrest Hotel

Qawra Coast Road, Qawra (2157 7101/www.suncresthotel.com). €€.

An abundance of white marble and brass, cascading water features and countless mirrors are just some of the touches of retro chic at the Suncrest Hotel. Its proximity to the action is a distinct advantage – Malta's busiest beaches are within walking distance, as are its most bustling beachside towns – while kids' areas complete with DVD players and daily activity workshops make it a good choice for families. Parents, meanwhile, can soak up the rays at the on-site lido, and there's a range of organised water sports on offer to hardier holidaymakers, including windsurfing, sailing and accompanied diving excursions off the nearby coastline.

Gozo & Comino

Comino Hotel

San Niklaw Bay, Comino (2152 9821/www.cominohotel.com).
Open Apr-Oct. €€.

This unremarkable brick-coloured building doesn't look like much from the outside, but the only hotel in Comino offers spacious en suite rooms with all the trimmings and, in a separate annex, a standalone cluster of bungalows surrounded by lush gardens.

Radisson SAS Golden
Sands Resort & Spa p147

ESSENTIALS

There are two outdoor pools – one for adults, one for children – and a pair of private beaches, although needless to say there's little competition for space from Comino's handful of tourists. There are various restaurants and bars, an internet café and a range of organised outdoor activities including tennis, diving and mountain biking.

Downtown Hotel

Europe Street, Victoria (2210 8000/ www.downtown.com.mt). €€.

This central hotel is set within a complex comprising a bustling café, a nightclub, a play area for kids and a small shopping mall, and as such is viewed by locals and tourists alike as much as a community centre as an accommodation option in the conventional sense. Rooms are modern, spacious and smart, with prices varying depending on the view. It's hardly the most upmarket hotel on the island, but it serves its purpose at an affordable price and seldom fails to entertain.

Electra Hotel

Valley Road, Marsalforn (2155 6196). €. No credit cards.

There are a dozen basic rooms at this popular budget hotel, which also happens to be one of Gozo's oldest, with a homely atmosphere and a quaint setting on the picturesque Marsalforn waterfront. A few of the rooms are singles with shared bathrooms, the rest are doubles with en suite facilities.

Grand Hotel

Mgarr Harbour (2156 3840). €€.

A small hotel offering pleasant, spacious and very clean rooms, most of them with balconies and with air conditioning and en suite bathrooms as standard. The hotel is busy in the tourist season and offers views over bustling Mgarr Harbour and beyond.

Hotel Calypso

Marsalforn Bay (2156 2000/ www.hotelcalypsogozo.com). €€.

On an island less notable for its architectural elegance, the Hotel Calypso stands out for its contemporary design.

The spacious rooms are made all the more soothing through a mix of blue and cream tones, and offer excellent views of Marsalforn's harbour and the Mediterranean beyond. There's also a decent outdoor pool and a smart deck area, both far more luxurious than other local hotels in this price category. The hotel café serves good food and bustles with activity most days.

Hotel Ta' Cenc

Sannat (2155 6819/www.vjborg.com). €€€.

Splendidly isolated and set in sprawling grounds, Hotel Ta' Cenc is surrounded by glorious gardens and the bars and restaurants are extremely spacious and smart. Rooms all come with luxury amenities and balconies afford extensive sea and country views, plus guests have access to a secluded private beach at Mgarr ix-Xini. Service is a cut above the average.

Kempinski San Lawrenz Resort

Rokon Street, San Lawrenz (2211 0000/ www.kempinski-gozo.com). €€€.

Undoubtedly one of the smartest accommodation options on Gozo, this large hotel complex is set in open fields on the western reaches of the island, and is designed around a large swimming pool and an elegant outdoor terrace. Wellness and leisure are a big part of the resort's attraction, with holistic treatments at the on-site spa and a range of packages for those hoping to make the most of it. There's also a good kids' club and various restaurants.

San Antonio Guesthouse

Tower Street, Xlendi (2156 3555). €.

This small guesthouse on the outskirts of Xlendi has 13 large rooms, most of them twins and a handful with double beds, air conditioning and an en suite bathroom. Friendly service and a quiet location make the San Antonio Guesthouse a pleasant and intimate place to stay, especially for families, although those seeking a more action-packed holiday may find it sedate.

Getting Around

Arriving & leaving

By air

All flights arrive and leave **Malta International Airport** in the central region of Luqa. The Maltese islands are only a few hours away from major European cities by air, with the national airline, Air Malta, operating flights to and from all major airports in Europe, North Africa and the Middle East.

Malta International Airport has a 24hr flight enquiry service (5004 3333) listing information on all its arrivals and departures. The online schedules (www.maltairport.com) are updated every five minutes.

It wasn't until the summer of 2006 that the budget airline revolution came to Malta, but a wide range of international low-cost carriers finally operate regular scheduled flights to and from Malta International Airport. Charter flights are also available.

Air Malta 2169 0890/ www.airmalta.com.
British Airways 2124 2233/ www.britishairways.com.
British Jet 2157 9350/ www.britishjet.com.
Alitalia 2123 7333/ www.alitalia.com.
Emirates 2557 7255/ www.emirates.com.
KLM 2134 2472/www.klm.com.
Lufthansa 2125 2020/ www.lufthansa.com.
Ryanair www.ryanair.com.
GermanWings www.germanwings.com.
Meridiana www.meridiana.it.
Click Air www.clickair.com.

Malta International Airport

Luqa (2124 9600/www.maltairport.com).

Located 8km (5 miles) south of Valletta, Malta's main airport has ATMs (HSBC and Bank of Valletta), a post office, phone booths, Wi-Fi (cards sold on site) and public internet kiosks.

Airport connections

Bus 8 runs every 30mins from the airport to Valletta (via Floriana) and vice versa (6am-9pm Mon-Fri; 6am-9.30pm Fri, Sat). Tickets cost €0.47. Taxis from the airport work on a fixed rate (it's €13.98 to Valletta, €18.63 to Sliema or St Julian's, €23.29 to Bugibba).

Those travelling to Gozo are well served by a Gozo Channel Company shuttle bus between the airport and the passenger terminal at Çirkewwa, from where ferries depart for Gozo (see Travelling to Gozo). Bus tickets cost €5, and timetables can be found at www.gozochannel.com.

By sea

A regular ferry and catamaran service links several Italian and Sicilian ports to Valletta. Several Maltese shipping lines also run services to a number of Mediterranean ports.

SMS Travel & Tourism 2123 2211.
Sullivan Maritime 2125 1564/ www.sullivanmaritime.com.mt.
Virtu Ferries 2122 8777/ www.virtuferries.com.

Car hire

Most international car hire companies have a branch in Malta. Local companies also hire cars – some even offer a chauffeur. Car hire rates are very reasonable compared to those in major European cities.

ESSENTIALS

Avis *Arrivals Lounge, Malta International Airport (2124 6640).*
Europcar *Arrivals Lounge, Malta International Airport (761000).*
Hertz *Arrivals Lounge, Malta International Airport (021 314636/7).*

City transport

Bus

The main bus station in Malta is in Valletta, just outside the City Gate. Buses in Malta are yellow with a distinct orange band and show the route number on the front. In towns and villages, the bus station is most generally found on or near the main square. In Gozo, it's in Main Gate Street, Victoria. Buses in Gozo are grey with a red band and also display the route number on the front. Unlike in Malta, Gozo buses operate on circular routes, leaving from and returning to Victoria with scheduled stops on the way. A regular service runs to and from Mgarr (bus 25), and is timed to coincide with the ferry timetable.

The bus system is based on a zoning structure, with fares from €0.47 to €1.16 depending on the zone. There are reduced rates for children and senior citizens. One-day, three-day, five-day and seven-day passes are available that entitle the holder to unrestricted travel, and cost €3.49, €9.32, €11.65 and €13.98 respectively.

Taxi

Taxis are usually all white Mercedes. All taxis are fitted with meters and should charge government controlled prices, although it's worth agreeing the fare before starting the journey. Taxis from the airport operate a different system; from here, you'll need to pay the fare at the taxi booth in the arrivals lounge. You will then receive a ticket showing the destination and fare paid, which

you hand to the driver at the end of your journey. Any complaints should be addressed to the **Malta Transport Authority** (2143 8475).

Cycling & sailing

Malta's roads aren't particularly well suited to cyclists – pot-holed and teeming with drivers oblivious to two-wheelers – but cycles can be hired at **Magri Cycles & Spares** in Mosta (2141 4399) or **Victoria Garage** in Victoria, Gozo. Cyclists will find the sister island's roads quieter, if no less uneven.

Those lucky enough to be able to sail to Malta under their own steam will find several marinas in which to dock, including Msida Marina in Valletta, Portomaso Marina in St Julian's, Cottonera in Vittoriosa and Mgarr Marina on Gozo. Contact the **Malta Maritime Authority** (2133 2800, www.mma.gov.mt) for more.

Travelling to Gozo

By air

A new seaplane, **Harbourair** (2122 8302, www.harbourairmalta. com), now runs between Malta and Gozo (€42 one way, €83 return). Flights operate between the Valletta Sea Terminal in Malta and Mgarr Harbour in Gozo from 1 April to 31 August. There are four flights to and four from daily (9.30am-5.30pm Malta; 10.10am-6.10am Gozo), all of which can be reserved online.

By sea

A regular roll-on/roll-off ferry service carries passengers and cars between Malta and Gozo, and takes about 30 minutes. For information and timetables contact the **Gozo Channel Company** at Mgarr (2155 6114), Cirkewwa (2158 0435) or Sa Maison (2124 3964), or visit www.gozochannel.com.

ESSENTIALS

Resources A-Z

Accident & emergency

For emergency services dial 112. The public general hospitals listed below both have 24hr accident and emergency departments. For police contacts, see p154.

Mater Dei Hospital
B'Karra Bypass, B'Kara (2545 0000/ www.materdeihospital.org.mt).
Craig Hospital
Victoria, Gozo (2156 1600).

Banks

Banks are normally open between 8.30am-1.30pm Mon-Thur, 8.30am-3.30pm Fri and 8.30am-noon Sat.

Credit card loss

The numbers listed below are 24hr.

American Express
00 44 1273 696933
Diners Club 00 44 1252 513500
Mastercard 00 1 636 722 7111
Visa 00 1 410 581 9994

Customs

Travellers from EU countries are not required to declare goods, so long as they are for personal use, up to the following limits:
- 800 cigarettes or 400 cigarillos or 200 small cigars or 1kg tobacco.
- Ten litres of spirits (over 22% alcohol) or 20 litres of fortified wine (under 22% alcohol).
For people arriving from non-EU countries the following limits on imported goods apply:
- 200 cigarettes or 100 cigarillos or 50 cigars or 250g tobacco.
- One litre of spirits or two litres of wine; one bottle of perfume (50g).

Disabled

Both the Maltese government and the private sector are working towards improving access for all to museums, attractions, cultural venues and the historic centres of towns and villages. Visitors may contact the Malta Tourism Authority (2291 5000, www.visit malta.com) to enquire whether a particular site or venue has easy access or facilities for the disabled. If assistance is required at Malta International Airport, the airline must be notified before the flight.

Commission for the Disabled
Centru Hidma Socjali, Sta Venera (2148 7789/www.knpd.org).
A governmental organisation that provides information on how best to get around the islands.
World Travel for Disabled Persons
9 New York Buildings, Qawra Road, Qawra (2157 0326/www.wtdp.org).
Holidays to Malta for disabled persons. Services include specialised accommodation, transfers and activities.

Electricity

Malta's electrical supply is 230 volts, 50 hertz. The three-pin rectangular plug system is used, as in Britain. Adapters are very easy to find.

Embassies

British High Commission
Whitehall Mansions, Ta' Xbiex Seafront, Ta' Xbiex (2323 0000/www. britishhighcommission.gov.uk/malta).
Open 8am-noon, 2-4pm Mon-Fri.
French Embassy
130 Melita Street, Valletta (2123 3430). **Open** 8.30am-1pm, 2-5pm Mon-Fri.

ESSENTIALS

German Embassy *First Floor, Il-Pjazzetta, Tower Road, Sliema (2133 6531).* **Open** 9am-noon Mon-Fri.
Italian Embassy *5 Vilhena Street, Floriana (2123 3157).* Open 9.30am-noon Mon-Wed, Fri; 9.30am-3pm Thur.

Health

Private and public hospitals in Malta are very modern and supported by a regional network of health centres. Visitors are advised to take out a personal medical insurance policy, particularly if they are not EU nationals. EU, EEA and Swiss nationals holding the European Health Insurance Card (which has replaced the E111) have access to Malta's public health service and are entitled to free medical and hospital care in both Malta and Gozo. Australians visiting the islands for less than one month are also entitled to free hospital care during their stay. Malta's private hospitals are listed below; for a list of public hospitals, see p153.

St James Hospital *Gorg Borg Olivier Street, Sliema (2133 5235/ www.stjameshospital.com).*
St Mark's Health Clinic *Clarence Street, Msida (2123 9488).*
St Philip's Hospital *Santa Venera (2144 2211/www.stphilips.com.mt).*

Chemists

Chemists are found throughout the islands and are open during normal shopping hours in the week. On Sundays they open 9am-12.30pm in Malta and 7.30-11am in Gozo.

Dental emergency

A full list of dentists can be found in the *Yellow Pages* under 'Dental Surgeons'. The public hospitals in Malta and Gozo provide emergency dental services for free to EU and EEA nationals holding the European Health Insurance Card.

Doctors

A list of doctors can be found in the *Yellow Pages* under 'Clinics – Private' and 'Hospitals – Private'. Expect to pay around €23.50 for a one-off consultation.

STDs, HIV & AIDS

The Genito-Urinary Clinic at the Sir Paul Boffa Hospital in Floriana (2122 7981) provides free professional help and advice, confidential diagnosis and the treatment of sexually-transmitted infections and related conditions .

Internet

There are internet cafés scattered throughout most of Malta. Most hotels have at least computer for the use of guests; some offer free Wi-Fi on all floors. Broadband, however, is less prevalent, and download times can be slow.

Lost luggage

In the case of lost luggage you should immediately get in touch with Malta International Airport (2124 9600), which keeps all lost property on site.

Opening hours

Shops are normally open 9am-1pm and then 4pm-7pm Mon-Sat. In more popular tourist areas, many shops remain open until 10pm. Public museums and sites generally have the following opening hours: *Oct-mid June* 8.15am-5pm Mon-Sat, 8.15am-4.15pm Sun; *mid June-end Sept* 7.45am-2pm daily. Final admissions are usually 15mins before closing time.

Police

Crime is low in Malta, but report incidents immediately to the police.

ESSENTIALS

The emergency number is 112 and the Police General Headquarters are in Floriana (2122 4001).

Mdina Police Station *(2145 4531).*
Qawra Police Station *(2157 6737).*
Sliema District Headquarters
Rudolph Street (2133 0502).
St Julian's Police Station
5 St George's Street (2137 2196).
Valletta Police Station
South Street (2122 5495).
Victoria District Headquarters
Republic Street, Victoria,
Gozo (2156 2040).
Vittoriosa Police Station
11 Desain Street (2182 5939).

Post

Most towns and villages have post or sub-post offices. Post offices in Malta and Gozo are open 7.30am-12.45pm Mon-Sat. Sub-post offices are open 8am-1pm and 4-6pm Mon-Fri, and 8am-1pm Sat.

Public holidays

1 January New Year's Day
10 February Feast
of St Paul's Shipwreck
19 March Feast of St Joseph
31 March Freedom Day
March/April Good Friday
1 May Labour Day
7 June Sette Giugno
29 June Feast of St Peter and St Paul
15 August Assumption of Our Lady
8 September Our Lady of Victories
21 September Independence Day
8 December Immaculate Conception
13 December Republic Day
25 December Christmas Day

Religion

Malta is a devoutly Catholic nation, but other religious denominations are also represented. There are small Anglican, Church of Scotland, Greek Orthodox, Jewish, Methodist and Muslim communities across the islands, and regular church services are held by all.

Smoking

No smoking is allowed in any entertainment establishment, including bars and restaurants, unless there is a designated smoking area. Smoking in public places is illegal and carries a hefty fine. Smoking is allowed at outdoor venues.

Sunbathing

The Maltese archipelago lies virtually at the centre of the Mediterranean and has a latitude even more southerly than that of northern Tunisia. You are therefore advised to take precautions to ensure you avoid overexposure to the sun at all times. Even in winter it is advisable to wear a suitable factor sunscreen for your skin type – this is all the more important if you are out walking or taking part in water sports. A sun hat is a must, and children and especially babies will need extra protection from the sun's rays. If you are intent on sunbathing, it is advisable to avoid the strongest sunlight when doing so – this tends to be found between 11am and 3pm in the height of summer.

Swimming

The Maltese coastal waters are generally clean and safe for swimming, and there are no tides. Some bays are exposed to north and northeasterly winds that produce strong undercurrents at times. Ghajn Tuffieha Bay and Golden Bay can both be potentially dangerous – a red flag flies to indicate when bathing should be restricted to only the innermost shallow waters. The sea temperature averages around 22.8°C in summer. For more on Malta's beaches, see p114.

ESSENTIALS

Telephones

Go (www.go.com.mt) provides 24hr international telecommunication, telex, fax and internet access at its offices in St George's Bay, St Julian's. Its offices in South Street, Valletta provides these services during office hours from Monday to Friday. The same services, as well as the sale of phone cards, are available 8am-10pm at Go's offices in Slicma, St Paul's Bay, B'Kara, Balzan and Malta International Airport. Go also offers a cheap international call rate from €0.035 per minute: simply dial 1021 before the country code from Go lines and payphones.

Tickets

Tickets are best bought directly from the venue itself, although tickets for a limited selection of events can also be purchased from www.maltaticket.com.

Time

Malta is on Central European Time (CET), which is one hour ahead of GMT in winter and two hours ahead between the last Sunday in March and the last Sunday in October. Malta is six hours ahead of Eastern Standard Time (EST) in winter and seven hours ahead between the last Sunday in March and the last Sunday in October.

Tipping

Tipping is generally expected in Malta. Tips are usually in the region of ten-15 per cent. As a rule of thumb: taxi drivers (not expected) should get up to ten per cent; porters should get €0.25-€0.50 per piece of luggage; restaurants, unless a service charge is added, should get ten-15 per cent.

Tourist information

Airport Tourist Information
Malta International Airport (2369 6073/4). **Open** 10am-9pm daily.
Malta Tourist Information
1 City Arcades, City Gate, Valletta (2123 7350). **Open** 8.30am-6pm Mon-Sat; 8.30am-2pm Sun.
Gozo Tourist Information
Tigrija Palazz, Republic Street, Victoria (2156 1419). **Open** 9am-12.30pm, 1-5pm Mon-Sat; 9am-12.30pm Sun

Visa

EU nationals and citizens of the US, Canada, Australia and New Zealand do not need visas for stays of up to three months. For EU citizens a passport or national ID card valid for travel abroad is sufficient; non-EU citizens must have full passports.

Websites

www.heritagemalta.org All you need to know about Malta and Gozo's heritage sites and museums.
www.visitmalta.com
General information on Malta and an updated calendar of events.
www.maltatransport.com
Official public transport website.
www.timesofmalta.com Online version of Malta's favourite daily.
www.um.edu.mt
Website of Malta's only university.
www.yellow.com.mt *Yellow Pages.*

What's on

Day by Day is a monthly magazine outlining major attractions and previewing forthcoming events across both Malta and Gozo. *Guide Me* is a glossier publication coming out once every two months and doing much the same thing, albeit with the blessing of the Malta Tourism Authority. To keep abreast of gay living across the islands, visit www.gaymalta.org.

ESSENTIALS

Index

ESSENTIALS

Eating & Drinking

ESSENTIALS

Time Out Travel Guides

Worldwide

All our guides are written by a team of **local experts** with a unique and stylish insider perspective. We offer essential tips, trusted advice and honest reviews for everything you need to know in the city.

Over 50 destinations available at all good bookshops and at timeout.com/shop

Time Out Guides